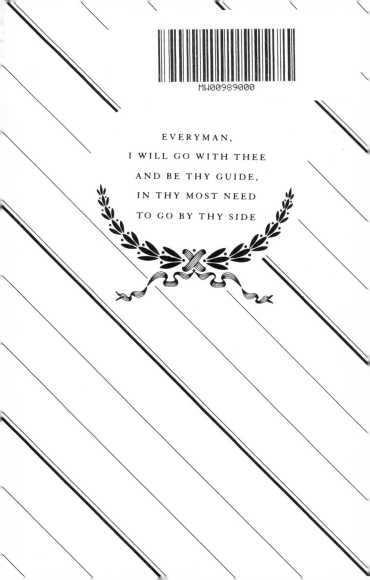

EVERYMAN,
I WILL GO WITH THEE
AND BE THY GUIDE,
IN THY MOST NEED
TO GO BY THY SIDE

EVERYMAN'S LIBRARY
POCKET POETS

CONVER-SATION PIECES

POEMS THAT TALK TO OTHER POEMS

••••••••••••••••

SELECTED BY
KURT BROWN AND
HAROLD SCHECHTER

EVERYMAN'S LIBRARY
POCKET POETS

Alfred A. Knopf New York London Toronto

THIS IS A BORZOI BOOK
PUBLISHED BY ALFRED A. KNOPF

This selection by Kurt Brown and Harold Schechter first published in
Everyman's Library, 2007
Copyright © 2007 by Everyman's Library

A list of acknowledgments to copyright owners appears at the back
of this volume.

All rights reserved. Published in the United States by Alfred A. Knopf,
a division of Random House, Inc., New York, and in Canada by Random
House of Canada Limited, Toronto. Distributed by Random House, Inc.,
New York. Published in the United Kingdom by Everyman's Library,
Northburgh House, 10 Northburgh Street, London EC1V 0AT.
Distributed by Random House (UK) Ltd.

US website: www.randomhouse.com/everymans

ISBN: 978-0-307-26545-6 (US)
1-84159-772-4 & 978-1-84159-772-0 (UK)

A CIP catalogue record for this book is available from the British Library

Typography by Peter B. Willberg
Typeset in the UK by AccComputing, North Barrow, Somerset
Printed and bound in Germany by GGP Media GmbH, Pössneck

CONTENTS

6

HE SAID, SHE SAID

9

REBUKES AND REBUTTALS

HOMAGES

FOREWORD

Poems should echo and re-echo against each other ... They
should create resonances. They cannot live alone any more
than we can.

Jack Spicer in a letter to Robin Blazer

At one time or another in the study of poetry, we are
likely to run into the notion that poems are not really
about love and death, separation and rapture and every
other human experience – they are about other poems.
At first, this may come as disappointing news. Poets, it
would seem, are not speaking to us; instead they are
speaking to their fellow poets, most of whom are beyond
earshot, that is, in their graves. That poets prefer the
audience of the dead to us living readers is not a flatter-
ing realization. But the broader truth of the matter is
that the past always plays a vital role in the poetry of the
present. As T. S. Eliot points out in "Tradition and the
Individual Talent," the only way poetry can be success-
fully written is in response to its own history. The real
reason why poets – or any writers – write is that they
have read and been moved to emulation. Poetry carries
in its arms the words of its predecessors. The writer's
page is illuminated by the candles of his past.

The poems in this anthology are a special breed,
poems that announce themselves as conscious, even

willful responses to other poems. They may take the form of answers to unasked questions, updatings, respectful nods, corrections, acts of sabotage, and rarely, works of adulation, but they are all intent on adding to the complex discussion that forms the long, ongoing history of poetry. A truth often lost on younger poets, who can be morbidly preoccupied with "self-expression," is that to write a poem is to become part of a Great Conversation. Poets need to listen to this conversation long and hard before they know what might be added. This talk among poets runs continuously back and forth through history, poets from all ages speaking at once in some great parlor of synchronicity. Whitman is talking to Ginsberg, but Ginsberg is talking back to Whitman. Christopher Smart speaks to Nicholas Christopher, and Philip Larkin talks back to Sir Philip Sidney. It is a party-line of almost infinite connections. We are used to thinking of a poem as an intimate communication between poet and reader, but a poem is also a public contribution to the body of past poetry. Poets are certainly speaking to their listeners, but they also are involved in a dialogue with a more exclusive audience, the inner circle of fellow practitioners.

The tones of the poems collected here are as various as the motives for writing them. The anthology includes paean poems, satirical attacks, deflations, game-like toying, piggy-backing, reproofs, send-ups, un-doings as well as delightful reconfigurations and revisions. Harold Bloom might consider such poems acts of aggression directed at a "father poem," as a way of relieving the anxiety that comes with being influenced by the shadow of a precursor falling across your page. But these poems may also be taken as acts of playfulness, symptoms of jealousy, or signs of a desire to be admitted into the club of poets. The tones change like musical keys, and we can rest assured that even though these poets may be talking to other poets, they want as many of us as possible to eavesdrop on what they have to say.

Billy Collins
Somers, NY

INTRODUCTION

This book began, appropriately enough, with a conversation — a dinnertime talk between two friends about some favorite poems. One of us had been savoring Hugh MacDiarmid's scorching reply to A. E. Housman's "Epitaph on an Army of Mercenaries." The other had just stumbled upon Byron's riposte to a little-known piece, James Montgomery's "The Common Lot."

We quickly realized that there was an entire genre of poetry that had never, to our knowledge, been represented in an anthology: poems that respond to earlier poems — that argue with, elaborate on, recast, poke fun at, or pay tribute to their inspirations.

In much lyric poetry, as Helen Vendler observes, we are, in effect, listening to the voice of a solitary poet addressing someone unseen, "someone not in the room" — a lover, a patron, a lost friend or family member. In the poems collected here, that invisible someone is another poet. As we read, we can hear one artist talk back to another in admiration or exasperation, praise or mockery, gentle rebuke or bitter disagreement. The monologue is suddenly transformed into a dialogue, the solitary meditation into an impassioned debate, the soliloquy into a conversation conducted across space and time.

Poems like these possess a special kind of magic.

They are, to begin with, delightful in themselves. Reading them is akin to hearing a jazz musician perform virtuoso riffs on a classic melody. To watch writers engage so intimately and urgently with their artistic peers is to get a thrilling sense of how vital, how *central*, poetry can be to our lives.

Beyond their own inherent virtues – wit, eloquence, passion, insight – these "response" poems cast surprising new light on the originals. No reader of Hugh MacDiarmid's piece, for example, will ever look at Housman's poem in quite the same way again. Other poems make us feel unexpected sympathy for La Belle Dame Sans Merci, ponder the aftermath of Leda's rape, and question the supposedly timeless wisdom of assorted literary masterpieces. Though we have avoided outright parodies, there are also plenty of chuckles to be had from poems like Ogden Nash's "Very Like a Whale" and Anthony Hecht's "The Dover Bitch" which expose the pieties and pomposities of revered classics.

The poem that inspired this entire tradition, of course, is Christopher Marlowe's "The Passionate Shepherd to His Love." Beginning with Sir Walter Raleigh's famous reply, poets through the ages have been unable to resist answering the shepherd's invitation. Four centuries later they are still writing back. We have therefore given Marlowe and his respondents pride of place in the anthology.

Poets who "talk back" to earlier poems have adopted different strategies. Some (like Raleigh) assume a persona, giving voice to a character who is silent in the original version. Some create sequels, letting us know (in Sharon Olds's phrase) "what lay beyond" the events of the earlier poem. Some engage in a direct debate with their predecessors. These and other approaches form the basis of our book's organization.

Kurt Brown
Harold Schechter

REPLIES TO THE
SHEPHERD

THE PASSIONATE SHEPHERD
TO HIS LOVE

Come live with me, and be my love,
And we will all the pleasures prove
That valleys, groves, hills and fields,
Woods, or steepy mountain yields.

And we will sit upon the rocks,
Seeing the shepherds feed their flocks
By shallow rivers, to whose falls
Melodious birds sing madrigals.

And I will make thee beds of roses,
And a thousand fragrant posies,
A cap of flowers, and a kirtle,
Embroidered all with leaves of myrtle.

A gown made of the finest wool
Which from our pretty lambs we pull,
Fair linèd slippers for the cold,
With buckles of the purest gold.

A belt of straw and ivy-buds,
With coral clasps and amber studs,
And if these pleasures may thee move,
Come live with me, and be my love.

The shepherd swains shall dance and sing
For thy delight each May morning.
If these delights thy mind may move,
Then live with me, and be my love.

THE NYMPH'S REPLY TO THE SHEPHERD

If all the world and love were young,
And truth in every shepherd's tongue,
These pretty pleasures might me move,
To live with thee and be thy love.

But Time drives flocks from field to fold,
When rivers rage and rocks grow cold;
And Philomel becometh dumb;
The rest complains of cares to come.

The flowers do fade, and wanton fields
To wayward Winter reckoning yields:
A honey tongue, a heart of gall,
Is fancy's spring, but sorrow's fall.

Thy gowns, thy shoes, thy beds of roses,
Thy cap, thy kirtle, and thy posies,
Soon break, soon wither, soon forgotten
In folly ripe, in reason rotten.

Thy belt of straw and ivy buds,
Thy coral clasps and amber studs —
All these in me no means can move
To come to thee and be thy love.

But could youth last, and love still breed;
Had joys no date, nor age no need;
Then these delights my mind might move
To live with thee and be thy love.

THE BAIT

Come live with me, and be my love,
And we will some new pleasures prove
Of golden sands, and crystal brooks,
With silken lines, and silver hooks.

There will the river whispering run
Warmed by thy eyes, more than the sun.
And there th'enamoured fish will stay,
Begging themselves they may betray.

When thou wilt swim in that live bath,
Each fish, which every channel hath,
Will amorously to thee swim,
Gladder to catch thee, than thou him.

If thou, to be so seen, be'st loth,
By sun, or moon, thou darkenest both,
And if myself have leave to see,
I need not their light, having thee.

Let others freeze with angling reeds,
And cut their legs, with shells and weeds,
Or treacherously poor fish beset,
With strangling snare, or windowy net:

Let coarse bold hands, from slimy nest
The bedded fish in banks out-wrest,
Or curious traitors, sleavesilk flies
Bewitch poor fishes' wandering eyes.

For thee, thou need'st no such deceit,
For thou thyself art thine own bait,
That fish, that is not catched thereby,
Alas, is wiser far than I.

SONG

Come, live with me and be my love,
And we will all the pleasures prove
Of peace and plenty, bed and board,
That chance employment may afford.

I'll handle dainties on the docks
And thou shalt read of summer frocks:
At evening by the sour canals
We'll hope to hear some madrigals.

Care on thy maiden brow shall put
A wreath of wrinkles, and thy foot
Be shod with pain: not silken dress
But toil shall tire thy loveliness.

Hunger shall make thy modest zone
And cheat fond death of all but bone –
If these delights thy mind may move,
Come live with me and be my love.

C. DAY LEWIS (1904–72)

RALEIGH WAS RIGHT

We cannot go into the country
for the country will bring us
    no peace
What can the small violets tell us
that grow on furry stems in
the long grass among lance shaped
    leaves?

Though you praise us
and call to mind the poets
who sung of our loveliness
it was long ago!
long ago! when country people
would plow and sow with
flowering minds and pockets
    at ease —
if ever this were true.

Not now. Love itself a flower
with roots in a parched ground.
Empty pockets make empty heads.
Cure it if you can but
do not believe that we can live
today in the country
for the country will bring us
    no peace.

30   WILLIAM CARLOS WILLIAMS (1883–1963)

LOVE UNDER THE REPUBLICANS
(OR DEMOCRATS)

Come live with me and be my love
And we will all the pleasures prove
Of a marriage conducted with economy
In the Twentieth Century Anno Donomy.
We'll live in a dear little walk-up flat
With practically room to swing a cat
And a potted cactus to give it hauteur
And a bathtub equipped with dark brown water.
We'll eat, without undue discouragement,
Foods low in cost but high in nouragement
And quaff with pleasure, while chatting wittily,
The peculiar wine of Little Italy.
We'll remind each other it's smart to be thrifty
And buy our clothes for something-fifty.
We'll stand in line on holidays
For seats at unpopular matinees,
And every Sunday we'll have a lark
And take a walk in Central Park.
And one of these days not too remote
I'll probably up and cut your throat.

OGDEN NASH (1902–71)

INVITATION

Come live with me and be my last
Resource, location and resort,
My weekday's focus and steadfast
Distraction to a weekend's sport.

Come end up with me, close my list;
Blank my black book, block every e-mail
From ex-loves whose mouths won't be missed;
Let nothing else alive look female.

Come couch with me *mit Freud und Lust*
As every evening's last connection;
Talk to me; prove the day like Proust;
Let what comes next rise to inspection.

Come, let old aftermaths get lost;
Let failures and betrayals mend.
Cancel repayments; clear the cost;
Once more unto the breach, dear friend.

Come lay us down to sleep at least,
Sharing this pillow's picture show;
Who's been my braintrust and best beast?
Who else knows what I need to know?

32   W. D. SNODGRASS (1926–)

COVENANT

To live with me and be
My love, proposing it
As if all the pleasures
Came to the same test,
Invites the love from living
In for life, deposing it
With an innocent lively
Tension of intent. And
To live with me *or* be
My love, selecting it
As if without the other's
Commerce the one could live,
Secures the life from loving
In live death, protecting it
With a deadly living
Waste of discontent. But
To love with me and live
My love, engaging it
One from the other neither
Leaving off, is to love
In the life of division
And live in loving it,
Where if loving only lives
It dies
But if living only will love
Then loving will live.

DOUGLAS CRASE (1944—)   33

WILLIAMS WAS WRONG

Now I find peace in everything around me;
in the modest campion and the shoals of light
leaping across the swaying sea
and the gulls gliding out of sight.
The tops of wave-confettied rocks
slide into water and turn into seals.
They move to the lively reel
of the cove's clapping dance hall,
rising blithe yelps above the sea's music.
The ocean draws in and out like an accordion
and unseen lithe fingers play the strings
of joy on what the moment brings.
The seals close and part and close again.
Their awkward fins have turned to wings.

VARIATIONS ON
A THEME

SPRINGTIME SLEEP

春 曉   孟浩然

春 眠 不 覺 曉
處 處 聞 啼 鳥
夜 來 風 雨 多
花 落 知 多 少

1. spring	sleep	not	aware-of	dawn
2. everywhere	–	hear	singing	bird/s
3. night	come	wind	rain	sound
(since last night)				
4. flower/s	fall	know	how	many

1. Springtime sleep: too deep to know dawn.
2. Everywhere, birds sing.
3. Entire last night: winds, rains.
4. Falling flowers: how many?

MENG HAO-JAN (689–740)

TRANSLATED BY WAI LIM YIP

SUMMER SLEEP
For Don Justice

Summer sleep   I missed the dawn
My tired eyes   too heavy to open

Far off birds argue   freeways hiss
Car alarms trill   false emergencies

In dream I am ten   napping in the Master's house
My single bed   a one-girl coffin

Too tight! I cry   *my feet can't fit!*
He scowls and sighs   scorns my mediocrity

Rain dances   death coins on the roof
Time devours us   imperceptibly

Empty womb   pupils beg for entry
Unfinished poems   don't know how many

SONNET 31
From *Astrophil and Stella*

With how sad steps, Oh Moon, thou climb'st the skies,
How silently, and with how wan a face!
What, may it be that even in heav'nly place
That busy archer his sharp arrows tries?
Sure, if that long-with-love-acquainted eyes
Can judge of love, thou feel'st a lover's case;
I read it in thy looks: thy languished grace,
To me that feel the like, thy state descries.
Then even of fellowship, Oh Moon, tell me,
Is constant love deemed there but want of wit?
Are beauties there as proud as here they be?
Do they above love to be loved, and yet
Those lovers scorn whom that love doth possess?
Do they call virtue there ungratefulness?

SIR PHILIP SIDNEY (1554–86)   39

SAD STEPS

Groping back to bed after a piss
I part thick curtains, and am startled by
The rapid clouds, the moon's cleanliness.

Four o'clock: wedge-shadowed gardens lie
Under a cavernous, a wind-picked sky.
There's something laughable about this,

The way the moon dashes through clouds that blow
Loosely as cannon-smoke to stand apart
(Stone-coloured light sharpening the roofs below)

High and preposterous and separate –
Lozenge of love! Medallion of art!
O wolves of memory! Immensements! No,

One shivers slightly, looking up there.
The hardness and the brightness and the plain
Far-reaching singleness of that wide stare

Is a reminder of the strength and pain
Of being young; that it can't come again,
But is for others undiminished somewhere.

40   PHILIP LARKIN (1922–85)

SAD STEPS

Piss

       off. The stars and the keen wind

by

       every measure should suffice,

cleanse

       a fisted night by rights. I

lied

       here, and here again. This

sky

       downwind of circumstance,

these

       palsied clouds, still on the go,

blown

       as though a sink would swirl and

part

       them, clogged and dull, down drains

below,

       dog on.

Separate

       stars seem, but so does the ringing

start

       of every chain I've clinked my skin –

no,

       clamped myself – into. Swinging

there,

       the meathead moon and its

plain

       dank cold ring

steer

       me nowhere. This thought the

pain

       spurs on. And then, in this late night,

again,

       the pissing comes so clear and clean

there

       follows the smallest softening.

"GO, LOVELY ROSE!"

Go, lovely Rose!
Tell her, that wastes her time and me,
That now she knows,
When I resemble her to thee,
How sweet and fair she seems to be.

Tell her that's young
And shuns to have her graces spied,
That hadst thou sprung
In deserts, where no men abide,
Thou must have uncommended died.

Small is the worth
Of beauty from the light retired:
Bid her come forth,
Suffer herself to be desired,
And not blush so to be admired.

Then die! that she
The common fate of all things rare
May read in thee:
How small a part of time they share
That are so wondrous sweet and fair!

EDMUND WALLER (1606–87)

ENVOI

Go, dumb-born book,
Tell her that sang me once that song of Lawes:
Hadst thou but song
As thou hast subjects known,
Then were there cause in thee that should condone
Even my faults that heavy upon me lie,
And build her glories their longevity.

Tell her that sheds
Such treasure in the air,
Recking naught else but that her graces give
Life to the moment,
I would bid them live
As roses might, in magic amber laid,
Red overwrought with orange and all made
One substance and one colour
Braving time.

Tell her that goes
With song upon her lips
But sings not out the song, nor knows
The maker of it, some other mouth,
May be as fair as hers,
Might, in new ages, gain her worshippers,
When our two dusts with Waller's shall be laid,
Siftings on siftings in oblivion,
Till change hath broken down
All things save Beauty alone.

DREAM SONG 171

Go, ill-sped book, and whisper to her or
storm out the message for her only ear
that she is beautiful.
Mention sunsets, be not silent of her eyes
and mouth and other prospects, praise her size,
say her figure is full.

Say her small figure is heavenly & full,
so as stunned Henry yatters like a fool
& maketh little sense.
Say she is soft in speech, stately in walking,
modest at gatherings, and in every thing
declare her excellence.

Forget not, when the rest is wholly done
and all her splendours opened one by one
to add that she likes Henry,
for reasons unknown, and fate has bound them fast
one to another in linkages that last
and that are fair to see.

MY CAT JEOFFRY
From *Jubilate Agno*

For I will consider my Cat Jeoffry.

For he is the servant of the Living God duly and daily serving him.

For at the first glance of the glory of God in the East he worships in his way.

For is this done by wreathing his body seven times round with elegant quickness.

For then he leaps up to catch the musk, which is the blessing of God upon his prayer.

For he rolls upon prank to work it in.

For having done duty and received blessing he begins to consider himself.

For this he performs in ten degrees.

For first he looks upon his fore-paws to see if they are clean.

For secondly he kicks up behind to clear away there.

For thirdly he works it upon stretch with the fore-paws extended.

For fourthly he sharpens his paws by wood.

For fifthly he washes himself.

For sixthly he rolls upon wash.

For seventhly he fleas himself, that he may not be interrupted upon the beat.

For eighthly he rubs himself against a post.

For ninthly he looks up for his instructions.

For tenthly he goes in quest of food.

For having considered God and himself he will consider his neighbour.

For if he meets another cat he will kiss her in kindness.

For when he takes his prey he plays with it to give it chance.

For one mouse in seven escapes by his dallying.

For when his day's work is done his business more properly begins.

For he keeps the Lord's watch in the night against the adversary.

For he counteracts the powers of darkness by his electrical skin and glaring eyes.

For he counteracts the Devil, who is death, by brisking about the life.

For in his morning orisons he loves the sun and the sun loves him.

For he is of the tribe of Tiger.

For the Cherub Cat is a term of the Angel Tiger.

For he has the subtlety and hissing of a serpent, which in goodness he suppresses.

For he will not do destruction, if he is well-fed, neither will he spit without provocation.

For he purrs in thankfulness, when God tells him he's a good Cat.

For he is an instrument for the children to learn
benevolence upon.

For every house is incompleat without him and a
blessing is lacking in the spirit.

For the Lord commanded Moses concerning the cats at
the departure of the Children of Israel from Egypt.

For every family had one cat at least in the bag.

For the English Cats are the best in Europe.

For he is the cleanest in the use of his fore-paws of any
quadrupede.

For the dexterity of his defence is an instance of the
love of God to him exceedingly.

For he is the quickest to his mark of any creature.

For he is tenacious of his point.

For he is a mixture of gravity and waggery.

For he knows that God is his Saviour.

For there is nothing sweeter than his peace when
at rest.

For there is nothing brisker than his life when in
motion.

For he is of the Lord's poor and so indeed is he called
by benevolence perpetually – Poor Jeoffry! poor
Jeoffry! the rat has bit thy throat.

For I bless the name of the Lord Jesus that Jeoffry is
better.

For the divine spirit comes about his body to sustain it
in compleat cat.

For his tongue is exceeding pure so that it has in
   purity what it wants in music.
For he is docile and can learn certain things.
For he can set up with gravity which is patience upon
   approbation.
For he can fetch and carry, which is patience in
   employment.
For he can jump over a stick which is patience upon
   proof positive.
For he can spraggle upon waggle at the word of
   command.
For he can jump from an eminence into his master's
   bosom.
For he can catch the cork and toss it again.
For he is hated by the hypocrite and miser.
For the former is afraid of detection.
For the latter refuses the charge.
For he camels his back to bear the first notion of
   business.
For he is good to think on, if a man would express
   himself neatly.
For he made a great figure in Egypt for his signal
   services.
For he killed the Icneumon-rat very pernicious by land.
For his ears are so acute that they sting again.
For from this proceeds the passing quickness of his
   attention.

For by stroking of him I have found out electricity.

For I perceived God's light about him both wax and fire.

For the Electrical fire is the spiritual substance, which
God sends from heaven to sustain the bodies both
of man and beast.

For God has blessed him in the variety of his
movements.

For, tho he cannot fly, he is an excellent clamberer.

For his motions upon the face of the earth are more
than any other quadrupede.

For he can tread to all the measures upon the music.

For he can swim for life.

For he can creep.

JEOFFRY THE CAT

The pale fields flow like the sea
in the darkening light.
Jeoffry keeps watch over me,
the two of us balanced
on the scales of the living God.
I drop to my knees
as the deadly moon alights
on the black hill
and the soft armies gather.
I see them there seeing me.
A man in London with a telescope
has cataloged my every sin.
Smart, Christopher. *Insanus.*
My heart is one star
he will never chart,
its lick of white flame blackening.
Jeoffry has seen the birds
of paradise in far galaxies,
the revolutions of dying suns,
the flickering angels in orchestra;
seen it all, unamazed,
in the fix of his jeweled eye.
I must not feed him meat or fowl.
Nor scraps of human prayer.
Nor slop of human desire.

Within these walls beating,
our two hearts merge
their singing chambers.
Our keeper, long fallen
to his present state, gapes
at me and asks what I scribble
each dawn staring southward.
A song of that red meadow,
I whisper, where the blind girls
dance their ancient step.
A song no one will hear.
Only Jeoffry hears the bells
that ring dark and light
in the fast skies of creation.
Jeoffry who licked the Baptist's head
And curled round Jesus' foot
by the lepers' well.
I am a mad Englishman,
more hound than jaguar,
more highwayman than cleric,
more brokenhearted than they suspect.
I eats my leavings.
I writes the pauses.
I bathes with hard wine.
Jeoffry he crosses this cell

fused with holy intelligence
and airy health,
his forepaws lifted
to the burning air.
When I die they must let him
to the road, his mission,
to grace the original rhythm
of the ringing of dark and light,
the glass road that spirals
and may not end,
that I shall never see.

ARRIVAL
After Christopher Smart

I will consider my son William,
who came into the world two weeks early, as if he
    couldn't wait;
who was carried on a river that gushed from his mother;
who was purple with matted black hair;
who announced his arrival not by crying but by peeing,
    with the umbilical cord still attached;
who looked all around with wide slate-blue eyes and
    smacked his lips as if to taste the world;
who took to his mother's breast right away;
who sucks my little finger with such vigor that it feels
    as if he's going to pull my fingernail right off;
who sometimes refuses my finger, screwing up his face
    in disgust as if I have stuck a pickled radish into
    his mouth;
whose face is beautiful and not like a shriveled prune;
whose hair, though black, is soft as milkweed;
who was born with long eyelashes that girls will
    someday envy;
whose fingernails are minuscule, thin and pliable;
whose toes are like caterpillars;
whose penis is a little acorn;
whose excrement is like the finest mustard;
who can squeak like a mouse and bleat like a lamb;

who hiccups and his whole body convulses;

who screams and turns red and kicks sometimes when
    we change his diaper;

who when he stops screaming is probably peeing;

whose deep sobs from the back of his throat bring tears
    to my own eyes;

who likes to be carried in a pouched sling;

who thinks he is a marsupial;

who has soft fur on his shoulders, back, and legs;

who is nocturnal and whose eyes are widest at night;

who will sleep sometimes if I lay him across my chest;

whose eyes flutter, whose nostrils dilate, and whose
    mouth twitches into strange grimaces and smiles
    as he dreams;

who is full of the living spirit which causes his body to
    wiggle and squirm;

who stretches his arms and arches his back and you can
    feel his great strength;

who lies with the soles of his feet together, as if praying
    with his feet;

who is a blessing upon our household and upon the
    world;

who doesn't know where the world ends and he begins;

who is himself the world;

who has a sweet smell.

"THE WORLD IS TOO MUCH WITH US"

The world is too much with us; late and soon,
Getting and spending, we lay waste our powers:
Little we see in Nature that is ours;
We have given our hearts away, a sordid boon!
This Sea that bares her bosom to the moon;
The winds that will be howling at all hours,
And are up-gathered now like sleeping flowers;
For this, for everything, we are out of tune;
It moves us not. – Great God! I'd rather be
A Pagan suckled in a creed outworn;
So might I, standing on this pleasant lea,
Have glimpses that would make me less forlorn;
Have sight of Proteus rising from the sea;
Or hear old Triton blow his wreathèd horn.

WILLIAM WORDSWORTH (1770–1850)   57

VARIATION ON A THEME BY WORDSWORTH

"When you're dead you're done," sings Ray Charles,
so we rock and roll long after nightfall. We woke
seeking in the sweating grasses at dawn the rising
gods of the earth, and we cheered beautiful Apollo
when he slowed his chariot to give us longer days.
But the sun bowed in shadow, and the pallid moon
lowered its face. I'd like to spot a few immortals
myself, now my time has grown short, so much
to be done and still the music of the spheres
in my ears. Nature was a sour smell of seaweed
and dead fish belly-up in the canal, but then
the sweet fennel by the path, and the wild clouds
of roses. And the sea never stopped sweeping
the ocean floor of wreckage and unspent coinage.

O TASTE AND SEE

The world is
not with us enough.
O taste and see

the subway Bible poster said,
meaning **The Lord**, meaning
if anything all that lives
to the imagination's tongue,

grief, mercy, language,
tangerine, weather, to
breathe them, bite,
savor, chew, swallow, transform

into our flesh our
deaths, crossing the street, plum, quince,
living in the orchard and being

hungry, and plucking
the fruit.

DENISE LEVERTOV (1923–97)

CASABIANCA

The boy stood on the burning deck
    Whence all but he had fled;
The flame that lit the battle's wreck
    Shone round him o'er the dead.

Yet beautiful and bright he stood,
    As born to rule the storm;
A creature of heroic blood,
    A proud, though childlike form.

The flames roll'd on – he would not go
    Without his father's word;
That father, faint in death below,
    His voice no longer heard.

He call'd aloud:– "Say, Father, say
    If yet my task is done?"
He knew not that the chieftain lay
    Unconscious of his son.

"Speak, Father!" once again he cried,
    "If I may yet be gone!"
And but the booming shots replied,
    And fast the flames roll'd on.

Upon his brow he felt their breath,
    And in his waving hair,
And look'd from that lone post of death
    In still, yet brave despair.

And shouted but once more aloud,
    "My Father! must I stay?"
While o'er him fast, through sail and shroud,
    The wreathing fires made way.

They wrapt the ship in splendour wild,
    They caught the flag on high,
And stream'd above the gallant child,
    Like banners in the sky.

There came a burst of thunder sound —
    The boy — oh! where was he?
Ask of the winds that far around
    With fragments strew'd the sea! —

With mast, and helm, and pennon fair,
    That well had borne their part,
But the noblest thing which perish'd there
    Was that young faithful heart!

FELICIA DOROTHEA HEMANS (1793–1835)

CASABIANCA

Love's the boy stood on the burning deck
trying to recite "The boy stood on
the burning deck." Love's the son
     stood stammering elocution
     while the poor ship in flames went down.

Love's the obstinate boy, the ship,
even the swimming sailors, who
would like a schoolroom platform, too,
or an excuse to stay
on deck. And love's the burning boy.

CASABIANCA III

Shifting on uncertain feet
He stands still trying to recite
In ardor, or perhaps stage fright,

Conflicting versions of his yarn
In voices that, reciprocally, burn
His post at school desk or at stern

Of sinking ship, that drown a crew
Blazing with envy, that torch the sea
In all its flaming complexity

With rhetoric itself, but leave
The boy whose stammer we forgive,
Who stands and stands for love.

BRUCE BERGER (1938–)

"I HEAR A RIVER THRO'
THE VALLEY WANDER"
From *Fragments*

I hear a river thro' the valley wander
Whose water runs, the song alone remaining.
A rainbow stands and summer passes under.

VARIATIONS ON A FRAGMENT
BY TRUMBULL STICKNEY

I hear a river thro' the valley wander
Whose water runs, the song alone remaining.
A rainbow stands and summer passes under,

Flowing like silence in the light of wonder.
In the near distances it is still raining
Where now the valley fills again with thunder,

Where now the river in her wide meander,
Losing at each loop what she had been gaining,
Moves into what one might as well call yonder.

The way of the dark water is to ponder
The way the light sings as of something waning.
The far-off waterfall can sound asunder

Stillness of distances, as if in blunder,
Tumbling over the rim of all explaining.
Water proves nothing, but can only maunder.

Shadows show nothing, but can only launder
The lovely land that sunset had been staining,
Long fields of which the failing light grows fonder.

Here summer stands while all its songs pass under,
A riverbank still time runs by, remaining.
I will remember rainbows as I wander.

JOHN HOLLANDER (1929–)   65

IN A STATION OF THE METRO

The apparition of these faces in the crowd;
Petals on a wet, black bough.

IN A STATION OF THE METRO

Some kind of trouble up the line somewhere, as yet unannounced, only its subtlest effects having arrived, premonitory. Absence gathers in the bedrock hush of a hall accustomed to an intermittent uproar. Utterly lost, a starling blunders from perch to perch, as if learning to fly, while we sit stiller and stiller, rehearsing our eventual departures. This hardly counts as travel, though, this hive-like circulation, this confluence and divergence of desires. The look we wear, most of us, because of the one woman who sits alone weeping loudly, messily, as if she would never stop, as if she had always been crying – the look we wear says, *I am not even here.* Against the wall stand three European boys with heavy packs. One, an Italian, is talking with obvious excitement; his companions listen, each wearing his northern skepticism like an elegant scarf. Behind their eyes, a cold swarm of Aristotle and Hegel, a string theory of critical theories in infinite regression, teeming, ramifying. They glance furtively side to side, awaiting the inevitable opportunity. We wait; the companions wait; only the starling, the weeping woman, and the Italian boy are not waiting, but plunging recklessly ahead, having now so little choice. The rails cannot believe their luck, as their daylong headache begins to ease, tentatively, miraculously; the tunnel blackens and deepens – or something worse than deepening, for depth implies a limit. Shifting from English to French and back, the boy now and then slips in a word of Italian in his excitement, then blushingly removes it. The sobbing is a bellows, ripping at the air, in and out; scored above it, a weak falsetto wail. The vowel is Russian, maybe, or Irish; the inflection untranslatable. Her hair hangs straight and lusterless, and her eyes are so swollen with tears she looks like the victim of a beating. A fistful of crumpled papers and a photograph. The boy's companions are no longer listening, they've demolished his argument, each in his own mind, and are ready to have at him as soon as he is done. Still virtual, hypothetical, the train is accumulating mass in some other realm, but the rails are singing in an ecstasy of relief. On the stairs, one of a pair of cops points his stick in the direction of the woman; they stand on spread legs, idly wondering whether to move, whether to bother. And then the mildest runner of pain shoots through the rails, gratifyingly familiar, and builds to an excruciating crescendo. In mid-thought, lips parted, the boy looks away from his friends – everyone looks up, squinting toward the light and ruckus. Everyone but the woman, who folds in around herself, and then flings her arms outward, scattering the pages and the photograph, which in the tumult of arrival fly everywhere, the pavement, the train, the bird, the surging crowd.

EL HOMBRE

It's a strange courage
you give me, ancient star:

Shine alone in the sunrise
toward which you lend no part!

NUANCES OF A THEME BY WILLIAMS

I
Shine alone, shine nakedly, shine like bronze,
that reflects neither my face nor any inner part
of my being, shine like fire, that mirrors nothing.

II
Lend no part to any humanity that suffuses
you in its own light.
Be not chimera of morning,
Half-man, half-star.
Be not an intelligence,
Like a widow's bird
Or an old horse.

70   WALLACE STEVENS (1879–1955)

MUSÉE DES BEAUX ARTS

About suffering they were never wrong,
The Old Masters: how well they understood
Its human position; how it takes place
While someone else is eating or opening a window or
        just walking dully along;
How, when the aged are reverently, passionately
        waiting
For the miraculous birth, there always must be
Children who did not specially want it to happen,
        skating
On a pond at the edge of the wood:
They never forgot
That even the dreadful martyrdom must run its
        course
Anyhow in a corner, some untidy spot
Where the dogs go on with their doggy life and the
        torturer's horse
Scratches its innocent behind on a tree.

In Breughel's *Icarus*, for instance: how everything
        turns away
Quite leisurely from the disaster; the ploughman may
Have heard the splash, the forsaken cry,
But for him it was not an important failure; the sun
        shone

As it had to on the white legs disappearing into the
    green
Water; and the expensive delicate ship that must
    have seen
Something amazing, a boy falling out of the sky,
Had somewhere to get to and sailed calmly on.

THE OLD AND THE NEW MASTERS

About suffering, about adoration, the old masters
Disagree. When someone suffers, no one else eats
Or walks or opens the window – no one breathes
As the sufferers watch the sufferer.
In *St. Sebastian Mourned by St. Irene*
The flame of one torch is the only light.
All the eyes except the maidservant's (she weeps
And covers them with a cloth) are fixed on the shaft
Set in his chest like a column; St. Irene's
Hands are spread in the gesture of the Madonna,
Revealing, accepting, what she does not understand.
Her hands say: "Lo! Behold!"
Beside her a monk's hooded head is bowed, his hands
Are put together in the work of mourning.
It is as if they were still looking at the lance
Piercing the side of Christ, nailed on his cross.
The same nails pierce all their hands and feet, the same
Thin blood, mixed with water, trickles from their sides.
The taste of vinegar is on every tongue
That gasps, "My God, my God, why hast Thou
        forsaken me?"
They watch, they are, the one thing in the world.

So, earlier, everything is pointed
In van der Goes' *Nativity*, toward the naked

Shining baby, like the needle of a compass.
The different orders and sizes of the world:
The angels like Little People, perched in the rafters
Or hovering in mid-air like hummingbirds;
The shepherds, so big and crude, so plainly adoring;
The medium-sized donor, his little family,
And their big patron saints; the Virgin who kneels
Before her child in worship; the Magi out in the hills
With their camels – they ask directions, and have
        pointed out
By a man kneeling, the true way; the ox
And the donkey, two heads in the manger
So much greater than a human head, who also adore;
Even the offerings, a sheaf of wheat,
A jar and a glass of flowers, are absolutely still
In natural concentration, as they take their part
In the salvation of the natural world.
The time of the world concentrates
On this one instant: far off in the rocks
You can see Mary and Joseph and their donkey
Coming to Bethlehem; on the grassy hillside
Where their flocks are grazing, the shepherds gesticulate
In wonder at the star; and so many hundreds
Of years in the future, the donor, his wife,
And their children are kneeling, looking: everything
That was or will be in the world is fixed
On its small, helpless, human center.

After a while the masters show the crucifixion
In one corner of the canvas: the men come to see
What is important, see that it is not important.
The new masters paint a subject as they please,
And Veronese is prosecuted by the Inquisition
For the dogs playing at the feet of Christ,
The earth is a planet among galaxies.
Later Christ disappears, the dogs disappear: in abstract
Understanding, without adoration, the last master puts
Colors on canvas, a picture of the universe
In which a bright spot somewhere in the corner
Is the small radioactive planet men called Earth.

MUSÉE DES BEAUX ARTS REVISITED

As far as mental anguish goes,
the old painters were no fools.
They understood how the mind,
the freakiest dungeon in the castle,
can effortlessly imagine a crab with the face of a priest
or an end table complete with genitals.

And they knew that the truly monstrous
lies not so much in the wildly shocking,
a skeleton spinning a wheel of fire, say,
but in the small prosaic touch
added to a tableau of the hellish,
the detail at the heart of the horrid.

In Bosch's *The Temptation of St. Anthony*,
for instance, how it is not so much
the boar-faced man in the pea-green dress
that frightens, but the white mandolin he carries,
not the hooded corpse in a basket,
but the way the basket is rigged to hang from a
      bare branch;

how, what must have driven St. Anthony
to the mossy brink of despair
was not the big, angry-looking fish

in the central panel,
the one with the two mouse-like creatures
conferring on its tail,
but rather what the fish is wearing:

a kind of pale orange officer's cape
and, over that,
a metal body-helmet secured by silvery wires,
a sensible buckled chin strap,
and, yes, the ultimate test of faith –
the tiny sword that hangs from the thing,
that nightmare carp,
secure in its brown leather scabbard.

BILLY COLLINS (1941–)

LAMENT

When I was a windy boy and a bit
And the black spit of the chapel fold,
(Sighed the old ram rod, dying of women),
I tiptoed shy in the gooseberry wood,
The rude owl cried like a telltale tit,
I skipped in a blush as the big girls rolled
Ninepin down on donkeys' common,
And on seesaw sunday nights I wooed
Whoever I would with my wicked eyes,
The whole of the moon I could love and leave
All the green leaved little weddings' wives
In the coal black bush and let them grieve.

When I was a gusty man and a half
And the black beast of the beetles' pews,
(Sighed the old ram rod, dying of bitches),
Not a boy and a bit in the wick-
Dipping moon and drunk as a new dropped calf,
I whistled all night in the twisted flues,
Midwives grew in the midnight ditches,
And the sizzling beds of the town cried, Quick! –
Whenever I dove in a breast high shoal,
Wherever I ramped in the clover quilts,
Whatsoever I did in the coal-
Black night, I left my quivering prints.

When I was a man you could call a man
And the black cross of the holy house,
(Sighed the old ram rod, dying of welcome),
Brandy and ripe in my bright, bass prime,
No springtailed tom in the red hot town
With every simmering woman his mouse
But a hillocky bull in the swelter
Of summer come in his great good time
To the sultry, biding herds, I said,
Oh, time enough when the blood creeps cold,
And I lie down but to sleep in bed,
For my sulking, skulking, coal black soul!

When I was a half of the man I was
And serve me right as the preachers warn,
(Sighed the old ram rod, dying of downfall),
No flailing calf or cat in a flame
Or hickory bull in milky grass
But a black sheep with a crumpled horn,
At last the soul from its foul mousehole
Slung pouting out when the limp time came;
And I gave my soul a blind, slashed eye,
Gristle and rind, and a roarers' life,
And I shoved it into the coal black sky
To find a woman's soul for a wife.

Now I am a man no more no more
And a black reward for a roaring life,
(Sighed the old ram rod, dying of strangers),
Tidy and cursed in my dove cooed room
I lie down thin and hear the good bells jaw —
For, oh, my soul found a sunday wife
In the coal black sky and she bore angels!
Harpies around me out of her womb!
Chastity prays for me, piety sings,
Innocence sweetens my last black breath,
Modesty hides my thighs in her wings,
And all the deadly virtues plague my death!

80   DYLAN THOMAS (1914—53)

LOVE POEM 1990

When I was young and shiny as an apple in the good
    Lord's garden
I loved a woman whose beauty like the moon moved
    all the humming heavens to music
till the stars with their tiny teeth burst into song
and I fell on the ground before her while the sky
    hardened
and she laughed and turned me down softly, I was so
    young.

When I was a man sharp as a polished axe in the
    polleny orchard
I loved a woman whose perfume swayed in the air,
    turning the modest flowers scarlet and loose
till the jonquils opened their throats and cackled out
    loud
when I broke my hand on her door and cried I was
    tortured
and she laughed and refused me, only one man in a
    crowd.

When I grew old, owning more than my share of the
    garden,
I loved a woman young and fresh as a larkspur
    trembling in the morning's translucent coolness,

her eyes had seen nothing but good, and the sun's gold
rolled off her wrists with reluctance, she pardoned
my foolishness, laughed and turned me down gently,
    I was so old.

And when I fell ill, rooted in a damp house spotted
    with curses,
I loved a woman whose bones rustled like insect wings
    through the echoing darkening rooms
and the ceiling dropped like a gardener's hoe toward
    my bed
so I stretched out my hand to her begging my god
    for mercy
and she laughed and embraced me sweetly, I was so
    dead.

BLACK STONE LYING ON
A WHITE STONE

I will die in Paris, on a rainy day,
on some day I can already remember.
I will die in Paris – and I don't step aside –
perhaps on a Thursday, as today is Thursday,
        in autumn.

It will be a Thursday, because today, Thursday,
        setting down
these lines, I have put my upper arm bones on
wrong, and never so much as today have I found
        myself
with all the road ahead of me, alone.

César Vallejo is dead. Everyone beat him,
although he never does anything to them;
they beat him hard with a stick and hard also

with a rope. These are the witnesses:
the Thursdays, and the bones of my arms,
the solitude, and the rain, and the roads...

CÉSAR VALLEJO (1892–1937)
TRANSLATED BY ROBERT BLY AND JOHN KNOEPFLE

VARIATIONS ON A TEXT BY VALLEJO

Me moriré en París con aguacero...

I will die in Miami in the sun,
On a day when the sun is very bright,
A day like the days I remember, a day like other days,
A day that nobody knows or remembers yet,
And the sun will be bright then on the dark glasses of
    strangers
And in the eyes of a few friends from my childhood
And of the surviving cousins by the graveside,
While the diggers, standing apart, in the still shade of
    the palms,
Rest on their shovels, and smoke,
Speaking in Spanish softly, out of respect.

I think it will be on a Sunday like today,
Except that the sun will be out, the rain will have
    stopped,
And the wind that today made all the little shrubs
    kneel down;
And I think it will be a Sunday because today,
When I took out this paper and began to write,
Never before had anything looked so blank,
My life, these words, the paper, the gray Sunday;
And my dog, quivering under a table because of the
    storm,

Looked up at me, not understanding,
And my son read on without speaking, and my wife
    slept.

Donald Justice is dead. One Sunday the sun came out,
It shone on the bay, it shone on the white buildings,
The cars moved down the street slowly as always,
    so many,
Some with their headlights on in spite of the sun,
And after a while the diggers with their shovels
Walked back to the graveside through the sunlight,
And one of them put his blade into the earth
To lift a few clods of dirt, the black marl of Miami,
And scattered the dirt, and spat,
Turning away abruptly, out of respect.

DONALD JUSTICE (1925–2004)   85

THINGS MY GRANDFATHER
MUST HAVE SAID

I want to die in the wintertime,
make the ground regret it,
make the backhoe sweat.

January. Blue Monday
after the holiday weekend.
I want it to be hard on everybody.

I want everyone to have a headache
and the traffic to be impossible.
Back it up for miles, Jesus.

I want steam under the hood, bad directions,
cousins lost, babies crying, and sleet.
I want a wind so heavy their umbrellas howl.

And give me some birds, pigeons even,
anything circling for at least half an hour,
and plastic tulips and a preacher who stutters

"Uh" before every word of Psalm 22.
I want to remind them just how bad things are.
Spell my name wrong on the stone, import

earthworms fat as Aunt Katie's arms
and put them under the folding chairs.
And I want a glass coffin,

I want to be wearing the State of Missouri
string tie that no one else liked . . . . God,
I hope the straps break

and I fall in with a thud. I hope
the shovel slips out of my son's hands.
I want them to remember I don't feel anything.

I want the food served straight from my garden.
I want the head of the table set. I want
everyone to get a pennant that says,

"Gramps was the greatest,"
and a complete record of my mortgage payments
in every thank-you note.

And I want to keep receiving mail for thirteen years,
all the bills addressed to me,
old friends calling every month

to wonder how I am.
Then I want an earthquake or rising water-table,
the painful exhumation of my remains.

I want to do it all again.

I want to die the day before something truly
important happens and have my grandson say:
What would he have thought of that.

I want you all to know how much I loved you.

THE ILLITERATE

Touching your goodness, I am like a man
Who turns a letter over in his hand
And you might think this was because the hand
Was unfamiliar but, truth is, the man
Has never had a letter from anyone;
And now he is both afraid of what it means
And ashamed because he has no other means
To find out what it says than to ask someone.

His uncle could have left the farm to him,
Or his parents died before he sent them word,
Or the dark girl changed and want him for beloved.
Afraid and letter-proud, he keeps it with him.
What would you call his feeling for the words
That keep him rich and orphaned and beloved?

WILLIAM MEREDITH (1919–)   89

THE INARTICULATE

Touching your face, I am like a boy
who bags groceries, mindless on Saturday,
jumbling cans of wax beans and condensed milk

among frozen meats, the ribboned beef
and chops like maps of continental drift,
extremes of weather and hemisphere,

egg carton perched like a Napoleonic hat,
till he touches something awakened by water,
a soothing skin, eggplant or melon or cool snow pea,

and he pauses, turning it in his hand,
this announcement of color, *purple* or *green*,
the raucous rills of the aisles overflowing,

and by now the shopper is staring
when the check-out lady turns and says,
"Jimmy, is anything the matter?"

Touching your face, I am like that boy
brought back to his body, steeped
in the moment, fulfilled but unable to speak.

ROOTS AND BRANCHES

    Sail, Monarchs, rising and falling
orange merchants in spring's flowery markets!
messengers of March in warm currents of news floating,
    flitting into areas of aroma,
tracing out of air unseen roots and branches of sense
    I share in thought,
filaments woven and broken where the world might light
    casual certainties of me. There are

    echoes of what I am in what you perform
this morning. How you perfect my spirit!
    almost restore
an imaginary tree of the living in all its doctrines
    by fluttering about,
intent and easy as you are, the profusion of you!
awakening transports of an inner view of things.

ROBERT DUNCAN (1919–88)

THE MONARCHS, 58

  Sleep, Monarchs, rising and falling
with the wind, orange children tucked in your
      winter bed,
teachers of patience and faith
    dreaming in the eucalyptus dark,
accumulating in your cells the photons that tell
you when to move, a sense
    I share in mind,
that makes the blue world
    light up, electric. It's too late

    to just let the world be and think
it will mend. Yet how you, little nothings, perfect
      my spirit!
    almost erasing
the actual ruin of living and all its doctrines
    with your evolved sleep –
delicate and frail as you are, the profusion of you
awakening in me soundings of the past
    that name the future.

HIGH WINDOWS

When I see a couple of kids
And guess he's fucking her and she's
Taking pills or wearing a diaphragm,
I know this is paradise

Everyone old has dreamed of all their lives –
Bonds and gestures pushed to one side
Like an outdated combine harvester,
And everyone young going down the long slide

To happiness, endlessly. I wonder if
Anyone looked at me, forty years back,
And thought, *That'll be the life*;
No God any more, or sweating in the dark

*About hell and that, or having to hide
What you think of the priest. He
And his lot will all go down the long slide
Like free bloody birds.* And immediately

Rather than words comes the thought of high
        windows:
The sun-comprehending glass,
And beyond it, the deep blue air, that shows
Nothing, and is nowhere, and is endless.

PHILIP LARKIN (1922–85)

IN THE MUSÉE D'ORSAY

When I saw them I knew right away
What they were like in bed,
Their lithe bodies fucking into
Heaven, both of them zipped up
In leather, her tall languid body
Leaning on his willowy frame –
Pasty skinned. As they looked
At the pictures, they were the picture
Of everything I'd not been.

I used to dream of that unlived life,
Rampant with rage I'd let it go by
Until I became a middle-aged wife,
And everyone who'd been my age joined me,

Kissing off that kind of happiness. I'd wonder
At the lost opportunities and what if...
But why didn't I? It wasn't about God

Or getting pregnant or even whispers – of what?
What stopped me from going to hell was
My will not to be taken, and now,
Stricken with sadness at the thought of this couple,
I wander through the museum under its pouring
    skylights,

And beyond, the noises of the street traffic,
    with the light
cumulous clouds, *fair weather* clouds streaming
    endlessly overhead.

MILKWEED

While I stood here, in the open, lost in myself,
I must have looked a long time
Down the corn rows, beyond grass,
The small house,
White walls, animals lumbering toward the barn.
I look down now. It is all changed.
Whatever it was I lost, whatever I wept for
Was a wild, gentle thing, the small dark eyes
Loving me in secret.
It is here. At a touch of my hand,
The air fills with the delicate creatures
From the other world.

MILKWEED

Remember how unimportant
they seemed, growing loosely
in the open fields we crossed
on the way to school. We
would carve wooden swords
and slash at the luscious trunks
until the white milk started
and then flowed. Then we'd
go on to the long day after
day of the History of History
or the tables of numbers and order
as the clock slowly paid
out the moments. The windows
went dark first with rain
and then snow, and then the days,
then the years ran together and not
one mattered more than
another, and not one mattered.

Two days ago I walked
the empty woods, bent over,
crunching through oak leaves,
asking myself questions
without answers. From somewhere
a froth of seeds drifted by touched

with gold in the last light
of a lost day, going with
the wind as they always did.

TRUE LOVE

In the middle of the night, when we get up
after making love, we look at each other in
complete friendship, we know so fully
what the other has been doing. Bound to each other
like mountaineers come down from a mountain,
bound with the tie of the delivery-room,
we wander down the hall to the bathroom, I can
hardly walk, I wobble through the granular
shadowless air, I know where you are
with my eyes closed, we are bound to each other
with huge invisible threads, our sexes
muted, exhausted, crushed, the whole
body a sex – surely this
is the most blessed time of my life,
our children asleep in their beds, each fate
like a vein of abiding mineral
not discovered yet. I sit
on the toilet in the night, you are somewhere in
        the room,
I open the window and snow has fallen in a
steep drift, against the pane, I
look up, into it,
a wall of cold crystals, silent
and glistening, I quietly call to you
and you come and hold my hand and I say
I cannot see beyond it. I cannot see beyond it.

SHARON OLDS (1942–)   99

WHAT LAY BEYOND IT

This
lay
beyond it. My spine
uncurls along the kitchen floor.
The cloud above the half-curtain
moves as if alive. My husband
is up inside this sky somewhere
on a short trip – not the hole he will
tear soon in matter. No one knows,
yet, that he is leaving me,
I am pulled along now through the days and hours
like a hooded figure on a float. Our son's
cat, tips of the ears first,
enters the kitchen, and steps up onto
my belly as if into a hammock, and rides
her human horizon. My hands move
on her, and the place that draws my touch
is the rich, nape rumple of skin,
and nerve, and flesh, that her mother was meant
to lift her by. Now that I am not
loved, I feel as if I am lying
in some antechamber, maybe near
the one where the unconceived wait,
or the one where the unborn wait,
or the one where the not-adopted wait,

and while I wait my nape is humming,
low contralto, as if to a light
sleeper – to my mother, or to the place in her mother
where my mother lay unloved.

HE SAID, SHE SAID

TWO FRAGMENTS

(41)
This crazy girl, so thoroughly fucked over,
demands that I should pay her her ten thousand!
That girl with the repulsive nose, the worthless
whore of the bankrupt Formian, Mamurra!
Now you – the girl's relations – you're in charge here,
you'd better call her friends & get the doctors:
she isn't well, this girl – and never bothers
to pause before a mirror for reflection.

(70)
My woman says there is no one whom she'd
    rather marry
  than me, not even Jupiter, if he came courting.
That's what she says – but what a woman says to a
    passionate lover
  ought to be scribbled on wind, on running water.

CATULLUS (84–54 BC)
TRANSLATED BY CHARLES MARTIN

SKIPPING THE STATE

Know I did not speak ill of you
when you left me weeping and pregnant
in the suburbs, for that girl with spiked hair
and a tongue ring. I have not defaulted
on the mortgage, or revealed to your enemies
your smoldering secret – how you liked it
when I pretended to have betrayed you with Robert
and you turned on the spit of minor-league jealousy,
the kind with no penalty, since you knew I was
faking. Nor in regard to naughtier longings
did I turn loquacious, nor list for other women

your shortfalls. Grant me, then, the child-support
payments, which, after all, result from your indulgence
and my gullibility, trusting that things you said
in private might be taken literally. Forgetting,
under the spell of your rhetoric, that declarations
men make while inside women
will be retroactively rescinded

on withdrawal. Though you, of all people, had the
        temerity
to question my fidelity – believe me, the child
is ours. In honor, then, of our son's innocence,
rise, please, to this fiduciary occasion.

AMORES III, 14

You're charming – misbehave then – I'll agree
So long as I, poor fool, don't have to see.
My morals don't require you to live chaste,
But just to try to hide it when it's past.
A girl has not done wrong who can deny it;
It's those confessing lose their good names by it.
What madness to reveal night's pranks by day,
And hidden secrets openly betray!
A prostitute performs in privacy
And sees the room is clear and turns the key.
Will you make shipwreck of your honest name
And let the world be witness of the same?
Behave yourself, or play the puritan,
And I shall think you chaste, do what you can.
Do what you do; just say it wasn't done;
In public, too, discretion never shun.

There is a place demands a naughty game;
Fill it with fun, fill it and feel no shame.
But when you're up and dressed, be staid and grave,
And in the bed leave all the faults you have.
Yes, take your clothes off there and don't be shy
Of lying close together, thigh to thigh.
There in your rosy lips my tongue entomb;
Practise a thousand love-games when you come.

There words of loving warmth don't fail to speak,
And with your pastime let the bedstead creak.
But with your dress put on an honest face,
And blush and seem as you were full of grace.
Cheat all, cheat me, so long as I don't see;
Let me enjoy my crass credulity.

Why do I see those notes received and given?
Why both sides of the bed left so uneven,
Your hair that more than sleep has disarrayed,
And on your neck the bites of love displayed?
Before my eyes all but the act I see;
If you won't spare your name, at least spare me.
It's death when you confess what you have done,
And through my veins I feel the cold blood run.
Then you, whom I must love, I hate in vain,
And would be dead, but dead with you remain.
The things you'd hide, I'll never search or sift,
To be deceived I'll value as a gift.
But if I ever catch you in mid-guilt,
And your disgrace is proved up to the hilt,
Deny I've seen what's clear as day, be wise,
And I will trust your words more than my eyes.
It's easy beating one who wants to lose;
Just say "Not guilty" – they're the words to use.
With those two words there's victory to be had,
So win the judge, although the case is bad.

108   OVID (43 BC–AD 17)
          TRANSLATED BY CHRISTOPHER MARLOWE
          MODERNIZED BY A. D. MELVILLE

COUNTER-AMORES, III, 14

I'm bad – but I behave – I contradict
myself – I never do what I depict.
I don't have morals, but I still live chaste;
I write the worst so it won't go to waste.
I don't lie down – but still a girl can lie
on paper – to remember someone by.
In sanity – a clean, well-lighted place –
I write things you won't read upon my face.
Brides and virgins need their privacy;
invite a crowd – there's nothing here to see.
(Honestly? This name was never mine –
if it becomes notorious – that's fine
by me – how many times has he had sex
since he became my once and future ex?
Let him assume I never sleep at night –
not that what keeps me up's this need to write.)

Nuns fret not at their convents' narrow rooms.
I'm not ashamed to fret. The wide world looms
so I lie down, under the fretful covers
and fret with all my dearly faulty lovers
who wander fully clothed at some remove
of minds and miles – they don't guess that they love,
or the proximity of lip & tongue
the infinite ways that we've devised to come,

the things I say he's never failed to say,
the mess we made of the sheets the other day.
Am I then so dishonest when I lie
all unashamed, because what haven't I
done with you – all that we haven't done
exposed here to the full light of the sun.

I lie with you, I lie for all to see,
enjoy such lying as allowed to me.
Material proof – what kind of evidence
(DNA, denial) – that's the president's
problem. If I say you're here with me
then here you are. And here. And heresy
the claim a heart might need more proof than this
or body confirmation of heart's bliss.
It's life when I protest what we have done
and through real veins I feel the hot blood run.
Then you, whom I can't have, I love as real
as life and twice as natural, I feel
you in my bones. I've nothing to declare
except my self – I'm duty free – I swear
I'm ninety-nine and forty-four percent pure
guilt – I only wish my guilt secure.
Could we do something that I couldn't say
or trust to paper? Dear, I'd seize the day.

TO HIS COY MISTRESS

Had we but world enough, and time,
This coyness, lady, were no crime.
We would sit down, and think which way
To walk, and pass our long love's day.
Thou by the Indian Ganges' side
Should'st rubies find: I by the tide
Of Humber would complain. I would
Love you ten years before the Flood,
And you should, if you please, refuse
Till the conversion of the Jews.
My vegetable love should grow
Vaster than empires, and more slow.
An hundred years should go to praise
Thine eyes, and on thy forehead gaze:
Two hundred to adore each breast:
But thirty thousand to the rest;
An age at least to every part,
And the last age should show your heart.
For, lady, you deserve this state,
Nor would I love at lower rate.

    But at my back I always hear
Time's wingèd chariot hurrying near:
And yonder all before us lie
Deserts of vast eternity.
Thy beauty shall no more be found;

Nor, in thy marble vault, shall sound
My echoing song: then worms shall try
That long-preserved virginity,
And your quaint honour turn to dust,
And into ashes all my lust.
The grave's a fine and private place,
But none, I think, do there embrace.
    Now, therefore, while the youthful hue
Sits on thy skin like morning dew,
And while thy willing soul transpires
At every pore with instant fires,
Now let us sport us while we may;
And now, like amorous birds of prey,
Rather at once our Time devour
Than languish in this slow-chapt power.
Let us roll all our strength and all
Our sweetness up into one ball,
And tear our pleasures with rough strife
Thorough the iron gates of life.
Thus, though we cannot make our Sun
Stand still, yet we will make him run.

COY MISTRESS

Sir, I am not a bird of prey:
a Lady does not seize the day.
I trust that brief Time will unfold
our youth, before he makes us old.
How could we two write lines of rhyme
were we not fond of numbered Time
and grateful to the vast and sweet
trials his days will make us meet?
The Grave's not just the body's curse;
no skeleton can pen a verse!
So while this numbered World we see,
let's sweeten Time with poetry,
and Time, in turn, may sweeten Love
and give us time our love to prove.
You've praised my eyes, forehead, breast:
you've all our lives to praise the rest.

ANNIE FINCH (1956–)

LA BELLE DAME SANS MERCI
A Ballad

O what can ail thee, knight at arms,
    Alone and palely loitering?
The sedge is wither'd from the lake,
    And no birds sing.

O what can ail thee, knight at arms,
    So haggard and so woe-begone?
The squirrel's granary is full,
    And the harvest's done.

I see a lily on thy brow,
    With anguish moist and fever dew,
And on thy cheeks a fading rose
    Fast withereth too.

I met a lady in the meads,
    Full beautiful, a fairy's child;
Her hair was long, her foot was light,
    And her eyes were wild.

I made a garland for her head,
    And bracelets too, and fragrant zone;
She look'd at me as she did love,
    And made sweet moan.

I set her on my pacing steed,
    And nothing else saw all day long,
For sidelong would she bend, and sing
    A fairy's song.

She found me roots of relish sweet,
    And honey wild, and manna dew,
And sure in language strange she said –
    I love thee true.

She took me to her elfin grot,
    And there she wept, and sigh'd full sore,
And there I shut her wild wild eyes
    With kisses four.

And there she lullèd me asleep.
    And there I dream'd – Ah! woe betide!
The latest dream I ever dream'd
    On the cold hill's side.

I saw pale kings, and princes too,
    Pale warriors, death pale were they all;
They cried – "La belle dame sans merci
    Hath thee in thrall!"

I saw their starv'd lips in the gloam,
   With horrid warning gapèd wide,
And I awoke, and found me here
   On the cold hill side.

And this is why I sojourn here,
   Alone and palely loitering,
Though the sedge is wither'd from the lake,
   And no birds sing.

LA BELLE DAME SANS MERCI

Her voice was songbird blue; her hair,
bedroom black, and men didn't know which
to love or which to fear. But when they
had to make a choice, it was what she
lacked they blamed her for, and so could
turn their backs guilt-free. If only
she could explain, it was all that singing,
it was all that wild honey, but more it was
those knights, one after another pulling her
onto the horse, asking her to sing – always
with that line, Has anyone ever told you...?
Then soon enough the two would come upon
that hillside where late in the day the dew
was stubborn, and here he'd beg for mercy.
Then sleep. Was it mercy they sought, or
pity? Later, she wasn't sure; she'd run out
of both for herself before she'd run out of
either for them. Even when there seemed to be
nothing left in her to give she managed
to find a drop or two of something – until
at last she'd given it all away, and when
the knight awoke, she was gone. Gone,
just like that! he told his friends
at The Mermaid. They nodded, full of pity,
and said they too had been victim of that
bitch, that tease. And the knight, feeling
so much better, ordered drinks all around.

MEG KEARNEY (1964–)

LADY CLARA VERE DE VERE

Lady Clara Vere de Vere,
    Of me you shall not win renown:
You thought to break a country heart
    For pastime, ere you went to town.
At me you smiled, but unbeguiled
    I saw the snare, and I retired;
The daughter of a hundred earls,
    You are not one to be desired.

Lady Clara Vere de Vere,
    I know you proud to bear your name,
Your pride is yet no mate for mine,
    Too proud to care from whence I came.
Nor would I break for your sweet sake
    A heart that dotes on truer charms.
A simple maiden in her flower
    Is worth a hundred coats-of-arms.

Lady Clara Vere de Vere,
    Some meeker pupil you must find,
For, were you queen of all that is,
    I could not stoop to such a mind.
You sought to prove how I could love,
    And my disdain is my reply.
The lion on your old stone gates
    Is not more cold to you than I.

Lady Clara Vere de Vere,
    You put strange memories in my head.
Not thrice your branching lines have blown
    Since I beheld young Laurence dead.
O, your sweet eyes, your low replies!
    A great enchantress you may be;
But there was that across his throat
    Which you had hardly cared to see.

Lady Clara Vere de Vere,
    When thus he met his mother's view,
She had the passion of her kind,
    She spake some certain truths of you.
Indeed I heard one bitter word
    That scarce is fit for you to hear;
Her manners had not that repose
    Which stamps the caste of Vere de Vere.

Lady Clara Vere de Vere,
    There stands a spectre in your hall;
The guilt of blood is at your door;
    You changed a wholesome heart to gall.
You held your course without remorse,
    To make him trust his modest worth,
And, last, you fix'd a vacant stare,
    And slew him with your noble birth.

Trust me, Clara Vere de Vere,
    From yon blue heavens above us bent
The gardener Adam and his wife
    Smile at the claims of long descent.
Howe'er it be, it seems to me,
    'Tis only noble to be good.
Kind hearts are more than coronets,
    And simple faith than Norman blood.

I know you, Clara Vere de Vere,
    You pine among your halls and towers;
The languid light of your proud eyes
    Is wearied of the rolling hours.
In glowing health, with boundless wealth,
    But sickening of a vague disease,
You know so ill to deal with time,
    You needs must play such pranks as these.

Clara, Clara Vere de Vere,
    If time be heavy on your hands,
Are there no beggars at your gate,
    Nor any poor about your lands?
O, teach the orphan-boy to read,
    Or teach the orphan-girl to sew;
Pray Heaven for a human heart,
    And let the foolish yeoman go.

THE ANSWER OF LADY
CLARA VERE DE VERE

The Lady Clara V. de V.
    Presents her very best regards
To that misguided Alfred T.
    (With one of her enamell'd cards).
Though uninclin'd to give offence
    The Lady Clara begs to hint
That Master Alfred's common sense
    Deserts him utterly in print.

The Lady Clara can but say,
    That always from the very first
She snubb'd in her decisive way
    The hopes that silly Alfred nurs'd.
The fondest words that ever fell
    From Lady Clara, when they met,
Were, "How d'ye do? I hope you're well!"
    Or else, "The weather's very wet."

Her Ladyship needs no advice
    How time and money should be spent,
And can't pursue at any price
    The plan that Alfred T. has sent.
She does not in the least object
    To let the "foolish yeoman" go,
But wishes – let him recollect –
    That he should move to Jericho.

HENRY S. LEIGH (1827–83)   121

THE VAMPIRE

A fool there was and he made his prayer
(Even as you and I!)
To a rag and a bone and a hank of hair,
(We called her the woman who did not care),
But the fool he called her his lady fair –
(Even as you and I!)

Oh, the years we waste and the tears we waste,
And the work of our head and hand
Belong to the woman who did not know
(And now we know that she never could know)
And did not understand!

A fool there was and his goods he spent,
(Even as you and I!)
Honour and faith and a sure intent
(And it wasn't the least what the lady meant),
But a fool must follow his natural bent
(Even as you and I!)

Oh, the toil we lost and the spoil we lost
And the excellent things we planned
Belong to the woman who didn't know why
(And now we know that she never knew why)
And did not understand!

The fool was stripped to his foolish hide,
(Even as you and I!)
Which she might have seen when she threw
      him aside –
(But it isn't on record the lady tried)
So some of him lived but the most of him died –
(Even as you and I!)

"And it isn't the shame and it isn't the blame
That stings like a white-hot brand –
It's coming to know that she never knew why
(Seeing, at last, she could never know why)
And never could understand!"

A WOMAN'S ANSWER TO *THE VAMPIRE*

A fool there was, and she lowered her pride,
   (Even as you and I),
To a bunch of conceit in a masculine hide –
We saw the faults that could not be denied,
But the fool saw only his manly side,
   (Even as you and I).

Oh, the love she laid on her own heart's grave,
With care of her head and hand,
Belongs to the man who did not know,
(And now she knows that he never could know),
And did not understand.

A fool there was and her best she gave,
   (Even as you and I),
Of noble thoughts, of gay and grave,
(And all were accepted as due to the knave),
But the fool would never her folly save –
   (Even as you and I).

Oh, the stabs she hid, which the Lord forbid,
Had ever been really planned,
She took from the man who didn't know why,
(And now she knows he never knew why),
And did not understand.

The fool was loved while the game was new
   (Even as you and I),
And when it was played, she took her cue,
(Plodding along as most of us do),
Trying to keep his faults from view
   (Even as you and I).

And it isn't the ache of the heart, or its break
That stings like a white-hot brand –
It's learning to know that she raised the rod,
And bent her head to kiss the rod
For one who could not understand.

LEDA AND THE SWAN

A sudden blow: the great wings beating still
Above the staggering girl, her thighs caressed
By the dark webs, her nape caught in his bill,
He holds her helpless breast upon his breast.

How can those terrified vague fingers push
The feathered glory from her loosening thighs?
How can body, laid in that white rush,
But feel the strange heart beating where it lies?

A shudder in the loins engenders there
The broken wall, the burning roof and tower
And Agamemnon dead.
                              Being so caught up,
So mastered by the brute blood of the air,
Did she put on his knowledge with his power
Before the indifferent beak could let her drop?

LEDA

"Did she put on his knowledge with his power
Before the indifferent beak could let her drop?"

Not even for a moment. He knew, for one thing,
    what he was.
When he saw the swan in her eyes he could let her drop.
In the first look of love men find their great disguise,
and collecting these rare pictures of himself was his life.

Her body became the consequence of his juice,
while her mind closed on a bird and went to sleep.
Later, with the children in school, she opened her eyes
and saw her own openness, and felt relief.

In men's stories her life ended with his loss.
She stiffened under the storm of his wings to a
    glassy shape,
stricken and mysterious and immortal. But the fact is,
she was not, for such an ending, abstract enough.

She tried for a while to understand what it was
that had happened, and then decided to let it drop.
She married a smaller man with a beaky nose,
and melted away in the storm of everyday life.

MONA VAN DUYN (1921–2004)   127

PANTOUM, WITH SWAN
For Carolyn Kizer

Bits of his down under my fingernails
a gob of his spit behind one ear
and a nasty welt where the nib of his beak
bit down as he came. It was our first date.

A gob of his spit behind one ear,
his wings still fanning. I should have known better,
I should have bitten him off on our first date.
And yet for some reason I didn't press charges;

I wiped off the wet. I should have known better.
They gave me the morning-after pill
and shook their heads when I wouldn't press charges.
The yolk that was meant to hatch as Helen

failed to congeal, thanks to the morning-after pill
and dropped harmlessly into the toilet
so that nothing became of the lost yolk, Helen,
Troy, wooden horse, forestalled in one swallow

flushed harmlessly away down the toilet.
The swan had by then stuffed Euripedes, Sophocles
– leaving out Helen, Troy, Agamemnon –
the whole house of Atreus, the rest of Greek tragedy,

stuffed in my head, every strophe of Sophocles.
His knowledge forced on me, yet Bird kept the power.
What was I to do with ancient Greek history
lodged in my cortex to no avail?

I had his knowledge, I had no power
the year I taught Yeats in a classroom so pale
that a mist enshrouded the ancient religions
and bits of his down flew from under my fingernails.

LEDA

He claimed no knowledge of that night.
But I could not forget the smack
that bruised and stunned, his appetite,
bill jabs on neck – cannot take back

what he had seized. I tried to reach
the god inside, batter his wings
with words, ignore his barb, his beak.
The beast gropes, guzzles, hovering.

He'll blame the drink, escape behind
the wine, the swan. Feathers inside
my mouth, I remain mute and blind.
A quickening before he flies.

He lives his lie. The bottle rolls.
I ache, cannot stand on the floor.
But my own kind will push to fight:
She'll throw a feast. She'll thrust a knife.

ZEUS: LEDA & SWAN

My dandy absurdity not only gave
access to the girl, but fascinated everyone.
Yeats with his politics, Spenser, Michelangelo
were all interested in the same thing.
Call it a problem: How would it work,
a girl with a swan? You have to realize
there are many things you never hear about,
that goddesses get boring. Or even mortals.
For example, I might have changed her to a swan.
Of course I could simply have swum to her,
my muscles gleaming . . . but straight sex has
        gotten dull.
There's nothing for me in that anymore.
I've taken the forms of most animals you could think of.
I am a source of what *you* call perversion.
They wait for me to come back, and they must do
        something.
It's made my world a lot more interesting.
You've never been with one of these?
I'm your god. Relax.

RICHARD FROST (1929–)

THE RIVER-MERCHANT'S WIFE:
A LETTER

While my hair was still cut straight across my forehead
Played I about the front gate, pulling flowers.
You came by on bamboo stilts, playing horse,
You walked about my seat, playing with blue plums.
And we went on living in the village of Chōkan:
Two small people, without dislike or suspicion.

At fourteen I married My Lord you.
I never laughed, being bashful.
Lowering my head, I looked at the wall.
Called to, a thousand times, I never looked back.

At fifteen I stopped scowling,
I desired my dust to be mingled with yours
Forever and forever and forever.
Why should I climb the look out?

At sixteen you departed,
You went into far Ku-tō-en, by the river of swirling
        eddies,
And you have been gone five months.
The monkeys make sorrowful noise overhead.

You dragged your feet when you went out.
By the gate now, the moss is grown, the different
    mosses,
Too deep to clear them away!
The leaves fall early this autumn, in wind.
The paired butterflies are already yellow with August

Over the grass in the West garden;
They hurt me. I grow older.
If you are coming down through the narrows of the
    river Kiang,
Please let me know before hand,
And I will come out to meet you
    As far as Chō-fū-Sa.

THE RIVER MERCHANT'S WIFE:
A FIFTH LETTER
After Li Po

My lord, it is both long and late
you have not written and gossip says
all passions dissipate.

Gossip adds you will not return to me.
Why should you with new worlds
spread, new roads before your feet?

Gossip says small loves, small fires die
with time and wind, although
huge fires and loves are magnified.

I tend the same fire we started.
I wait. But no letters from you.
My lord, I too am being courted.

I say this to hurry up your news.
It may or may not be true.

134   DIANA DER HOVANESSIAN (1934–)

THE RIVER MERCHANT:
A LETTER HOME

Sometimes the world seems so large,
You have no idea. Out here at dusk
The barges pull the heaviest cargo, sometimes
They drag whole ships to the sea. Imagine
The sound of geese shrieking everywhere,
More geese than you can imagine,
Clustered together and flapping like stars.
Sometimes there are two moons shining at
Once, one clouded in the treetops, one
Breaking into shadows on the river.
I don't know what this means.
But from the hill's brow I can see
The lights in every village flickering on,
One by one, but slowly, like this,
Until the whole world gleams
Like small coins. Believe me:
There are so many villages like ours,
So many lights all gleaming together
But all separate too, like those moons.
It is too much. I am older now.
I want to return to that fateful place
Where the river narrows toward home.

EDWARD HIRSCH (1950–)   135

"WHAT LIPS MY LIPS HAVE KISSED"
SONNET XLII

What lips my lips have kissed, and where, and why,
I have forgotten, and what arms have lain
Under my head till morning; but the rain
Is full of ghosts tonight, that tap and sigh
Upon the glass and listen for reply,
And in my heart there stirs a quiet pain
For unremembered lads that not again
Will turn to me at midnight with a cry.
Thus in the winter stands the lonely tree,
Nor knows what birds have vanished one by one,
Yet knows its boughs more silent than before:
I cannot say what loves have come and gone,
I only know that summer sang in me
A little while, that in me sings no more.

AFTER EDNA ST. VINCENT MILLAY

When I saw you again, distant, sparrow-boned
under the elegant clothes you wear in your life
    without me,
I thought, No, No, let her be the one
this time to look up at an oblivious me.
Let her find the edge of the cliff with her foot,
blindfolded. Let her be the one struck by lightning
of the other so that the heart is jolted
from the ribs and the rest of the body is nothing
but ash. It's a sad familiar story
I wish you were telling me with this shabby excuse:
I never loved you anymore
than I hated myself for loving you.

And about that other guy by your side
you left me for: I hope he dies.

BRUCE SMITH (1946–)

THE YOUNG HOUSEWIFE

At ten A.M. the young housewife
moves about in negligee behind
the wooden walls of her husband's house.
I pass solitary in my car.

Then again she comes to the curb
to call the ice-man, fish-man, and stands
shy, uncorseted, tucking in
stray ends of hair, and I compare her
to a fallen leaf.

The noiseless wheels of my car
rush with a crackling sound over
dried leaves as I bow and pass smiling.

138   WILLIAM CARLOS WILLIAMS (1883–1963)

THE YOUNG DOCTOR (1916)

He smiles and nods
as he drives by
thinking perhaps soon
she will be pregnant
coming to me
but he's wrong.
He sees a long line
of pregnant women
packed like fish
in a net bursting out
the seams of their dresses.
Ah. Give me a cup
of tea and a back rub.
Blood slime cupids cherubs, no thanks.
Give me trees losing their leaves.
I'm okay. I pay the ice man
and he brings ice
into the dark house
inserts the block of it
into the icebox
a dark womb of art,
while church bells dong dong
scaring the mice.
"Then again" as the fish man's nag
comes towing an old wagon

of trout, I turn about
to see who's driving by
and it's he, no lazy he,
I'm beginning to think
driving out of his way
maybe at least a mile
just to smile at me.
But no, that's crazy.
Against distant thunder
I watch my trout of many blues
being wrapped in trodden newspaper
and blundered by shaky hands.
And I understand.

FABLE OF THE MERMAID
AND THE DRUNKS

All these gentlemen were there inside
when she entered, utterly naked.
They had been drinking, and began to spit at her.
Recently come from the river, she understood nothing.
She was a mermaid who had lost her way.
The taunts flowed over her glistening flesh.
Obscenities drenched her golden breasts.
A stranger to tears, she did not weep.
A stranger to clothes, she did not dress.
They pocked her with cigarette ends and with
      burnt corks,
and rolled on the tavern floor with laughter.
She did not speak, since speech was unknown to her.
Her eyes were the colour of faraway love,
her arms were matching topazes.
Her lips moved soundlessly in coral light,
and ultimately, she left by that door.
Scarcely had she entered the river than she was cleansed,
gleaming once more like a white stone in the rain;
and without a backward look, she swam once more,
swam toward nothingness, swam to her dying.

PABLO NERUDA (1904–73)   141

THE MERMAID TAKES ISSUE
WITH THE FABLE
After Neruda

I came into the tavern totally naked, that's true.
And those drunk men inside: began to spit.
I was from the sea and I knew a thing, or two.
Yes, yes, a mermaid, but I had not lost my way.
The insults bounced off my gleaming scales.
Obscenities reflected in my tawny breasts.
Oh, I know tears, but on this we agree: I did not
        weep tears.
I know clothes, and I did not have clothes.
They blackened me with burnt corks and cigarette stubs
and rolled around laughing on the tavern floor, yes.
I did not speak because they would not have listened.
My eyes were the colour of close hatred.
My arms made of white diamonds.
My lips moved, a whisper, in light of the anemone
darts, white threads centered and caught by each
        gaping mouth.
Entering the sea I was rinsed
clear like an empty mug of beer.
And without looking I swam,
swam towards fullness, swam towards life.

WOMEN

Women are very distant. Their bedsheets smell of
　　good-night.
They leave bread on the table so we won't feel
　　they've gone.
Then we understand we were to blame. We get up
　　from the chair and say:
"You've overtired yourself today," or "Don't bother,
　　I'll light the lamp myself."

When we strike a match, she turns slowly and goes
toward the kitchen with an inexplicable concentration.
　　Her back
is a sad, small mountain laden with many dead –
the family dead, her dead, and your own death.
You hear the old floorboards creaking under her
　　footsteps,
you hear the dishes weeping in the dishracks, and then
　　that train
is heard taking soldiers to the front.

YANNIS RITSOS (1909–90)　　　　　　　　143
TRANSLATED BY KIMON FRIAR

MEN
After Ritsos

Men are very distant.
Their cars smell of goodbye.
They set the money on the table
so that we don't feel their absence.

Men are like packages
you don't want to open,
or books you can't allow
yourself to read.

They sleep in black yak-hair tents
and hunt blue sheep.
They stay in motor courts
and drink cheap whiskey.

Men live inside maps
and have eyes like gas flames.
It's amazing what they can burn
with one match.

MISSING

*Frank was missing something, and women would do
anything to find out what it was.*

— James Salter

He disappeared, often, even as he was speaking,
though he could finish those sentences
from which he had disengaged himself,
finish them well. And when I spoke
he was interested just enough to make me
want to continue speaking. Strange,
that I was flattered by this; it seemed
he was giving me all of half of himself,
the best he could do.
                        In bed, after lovemaking,
which was always good, I knew he'd learned
his post-coital manners – caring, tender –
and was performing them. I was sure
he was planning his next day, his secret
heart checking its secret watch.
I'd known other men like this, of course,
but he was so poor at concealing these faults,
and would admit to them if asked,
they seemed part of his presence, part of
the way he was always *there* for me,
if you know what I mean.

                        I felt, in time,
I could locate, perhaps give life to
his missing half. I felt love could do this.
And I felt even an odd love for his vacancies,
the way, I suppose, most of us will kiss
a terrible scar to prove we can live with it.
He had a good job. Men admired him
because he brought the entire half of himself
to work every day, brought it with intelligence
and charm. It was enough for them.
And all my women friends adored him,
said how lucky I was.
                        But I must admit
it isn't easy to love a man like him.
There's so little asked of you; after a while
you forget you're using half of yourself,
and then something reminds you
and an enormous sense of deprivation follows,
then anger — a quiet fury, I'd call it.
Which is why, finally, I left.
But I've never stopped wondering about him.
And I'm past my anger. If he walked in
right now, I think I'd put my arms around him
and breathe him in, ask him how he was.

AN EXPLANATION

Frank was missing something, and women would do
anything to find out what it was.
                                        — James Salter

It's nothing, really, just a kind of trick I use
to keep them. I look up from their bodies

with a tenderness I've maintained after we've made love
wishing to extend even further

that welcome moment of grace that settles in
just after the inevitable diminishment

over which neither of us has any control.
I look up from their bodies and glance

toward a window, if there is a window,
or a closet door or a calendar on the wall, perhaps

a candle on the bedside table with its rarefied flame.
If there's a painting above the bed, I make sure it's safe

before we even begin to undress or lie down
to undress one another. Once

it was one of those portraits of Jesus
naked and bleeding, which ruined everything.

I'm all there when I'm there. Yet sometimes, I've learned,
it's better to lift them out of themselves by giving

a little bit less. I don't mean to be cruel,
cutting them off from my pure attention. I only want

the deepest they'll give me, the thing you can't ask for —
they don't know where it is themselves. I think

of Valentino who was forced to use only his eyes to speak
and his body, the sound of his voice kept irretrievably

from us, that incomplete circle that wanted finishing,
and we, of course, supplied the best.

That's it, really. Leaving something necessary
out that they'll fill in. Something small, of course,

but important, something at first you don't withhold
so they'll notice right away when you do.

Remember the page in the children's magazine
that displayed a kitchen or a yard and asked you to find

the ten things wrong? An upside-down
clock, say, or a dog in a tree?

It's taken me years to learn this, and it works.
A woman will nest herself for as long as I want her.

She gives me more and more of everything, tries
to fill my gaps, plug holes in my conversation.

When she finally tires of her own failures, and leaves,
it never hurts. I always have at least her sympathies

and her longing. There are so many beautiful women
lighting this world. It's the only way I've found

to possess them.

ANDREA HOLLANDER BUDY (1947–)

A POEM BY MARY RUEFLE

It is a mistake to hope
my treatise will ever be unfolded.
I do not understand napkins myself.
I was by a mailbox not my own
when this thought hit me although
I was in no way actually hit
or slugged, stapled, set upon the wheel,
devoured by pigs, fed into the chipper-shredder.
The pains I have are nothing
compared to yours. Petite agons
the French say who concluded, afterall,
that burning the sugar is not an end
but a beginning. The unhurried
days, it is as if my flashcards
have gone half blank. Cosmic rays –
no definition, no snug equation.
Listz – who the hell was he?
And my mind, as any gas
exposed to fluctuations in pressure
is wont to do, heaves a sigh.
It is a mistake to hope
but not a biggie. A sad term on earth:
a conversation through a bathroom door,
the wrong tool almost out of reach,
codes punched in aluminum plates,

probably a misdemeanor. Thus
the wounds are received
one upon another, my other.
It is not pain that enobles us.
Smoke in the breeze, howling in the wood.
All afternoon sun strikes these steps
and now they are warm in the dark.

A POEM BY DEAN YOUNG

Don't think for one fucking instant
that I don't have a broken heart.
The man in briefs in an infinite sea
believes there is no subconscious
nor is he aware that tempora exists.
Don't think I have not eaten
in the most beautiful Chinese restaurant
in the world. Don't think I have not written
on the walls of my bathtub.
Don't think I haven't poisoned a snail.
Don't think I haven't ignited
the sulfur of the fortune teller.
Of course I have written a poem by Dean Young!
More than once I have written a poem by Dean Young.
More than once I have left them by your gate.
More than once I have stuffed the eucalyptus leaves
in your mouth. More than once I have lived,
more than once I have died because of it.
I love you. This remarkable statement
has appeared on earth to substantiate the clams.
Perhaps now we can reach an agreement in the
        Himalayas,
returning shortly thereafter as gods, the kind kind
largely ignored by larger and more sensitive organisms.
Don't think I wasn't shocked when
you were a traffic signal
and I a woodpecker.

REBUKES AND REBUTTALS

UNMARKED BOXES

Don't grieve. Anything you lose comes round
in another form. The child weaned from mother's milk
now drinks wine and honey mixed.

God's joy moves from unmarked box to unmarked box,
from cell to cell. As rainwater, down into flowerbed.
As roses, up from ground.
Now it looks like a plate of rice and fish,
now a cliff covered with vines,
now a horse being saddled.
It hides within these,
till one day it cracks them open.

Part of the self leaves the body when we sleep
and changes shape. You might say, "Last night
I was a cypress tree, a small bed of tulips,
a field of grapevines." Then the phantasm goes away.
You're back in the room.
I don't want to make anyone fearful.
Hear what's behind what I say.

Tatatumtum tatum tatadum.
There's the light gold of wheat in the sun
and the gold of bread made from that wheat.
I have neither. I'm only talking about them,

as a town in the desert looks up
at stars on a clear night.

RUMI (1207–73)   155
VERSION BY COLEMAN BARKS

RUMINATIONS ON MY VERY MINOR RUNNING INJURY

Rumi's poem, penned, crumpled, pinned to the
      pantry door:
I elbow-graze it, unmarked, as I snap the light on;
it greets me with its silence, swaying on its tack.
"God's joy moves from unmarked box to unmarked box."

The yellowed page, in motion, teases my attention.
It, at least, can to and fro, as can God's joy,
while I reptile my way forward, abducted by pain,
wobble, glass-fragile, to where the dishes are stacked.

I pour detergent beads onto scrub-brush to explore
brine-coated lobster cauldrons. Crustacean shards
      surround,
inert backhoes, their hinged scoops no longer dragging
deep, with jointed determination slow, slow; a lesson.

Unread, unmarked, this poem has languished.
      Patient guest,
that waterpocked page begins: *"Don't grieve."*
But why shouldn't I froth up my grief, friend, to buff
my pity-coins? We all hoard those counterfeits. Rumi,

spare me poems wishing losses return as blessings,
Zinnias sprouting from compost piles. My disinclined
limbs angle their listless pose before the sink,
while you, oh Crumbs, graciously succumb

to my sponge's sweep, and you, Black Marble,
glisten. *"God's joy moves from unmarked box
to unmarked box."* I daydream I'm in God's unattended
mailroom of boxes, boxes, stacked, precarious.

I stretch to open one, the pile atumble,
To find a humble English word,
     [bubblewrapped]
in its box, *"tatatumtum tatum tatadum,"*
then, quick, open another, shell game of God's joy.

Oh so sorry, the contents, curdled by inattention,
globs onto my counter, just sponged. That blissful
word *move*, grief to my limbs. It taunts me
as a neglected mistress: why was my spirit

not moved to her glories before? I edge, not move,
to reach that wineglass stuffed with Granny Smith core.
God's joy? It can't go in the dishwasher, for delicate
ringing rims do not endure. *The crystal glass*

resounds in its box like bones
of a timid poltergeist; with it shall we see far,
or near, or just drink to God's joy?
Say Rumi, have you already moved on?

"As rainwater down into the flowerbed" (God's joy)
"As roses up from the ground" (God's joy). *"Now it looks like
a plate of rice and fish"* (actually it's lobster)
"Now cliff covered with vines, now a horse being saddled."

"It hides within these." (God's joy). But Rumi: even
boxes marked **Regrets**? When we dare open
those, will we find instead, sun-coins
of God's joy: finches swinging on flower stalks?

THE COMMON LOT

A Birthday Meditation, during a solitary Winter Walk, of seven Miles, between a village in Derbyshire and Sheffield, when the Ground was covered with Snow, the Sky serene, and the Morning Air intensely pure.

— November 4, 1805

Once in the flight of ages past,
There lived a man: — and WHO was HE?
— Mortal! howe'er thy lot be cast,
That Man resembled Thee.

Unknown the region of his birth,
The land in which he died unknown:
His name has perish'd from the earth;
This truth survives alone: —

That joy and grief, and hope and fear,
Alternate triumph'd in his breast;
His bliss and woe, — a smile, a tear!
— Oblivion hides the rest.

The bounding pulse, the languid limb,
The changing spirits' rise and fall;
We know that these were felt by him,
For these are felt by all.

He suffer'd, – but his pangs are o'er;
Enjoy'd, – but his delights are fled;
Had friends, – his friends are now no more;
And foes, – his foes are dead.

He loved, – but whom he loved, the grave
Hath lost in its unconscious womb:
O, she was fair! – but nought could save
Her beauty from the tomb.

He saw whatever thou hast seen;
Encounter'd all that troubles thee:
He was – whatever thou hast been;
He is – what thou shalt be.

The rolling seasons, day and night,
Sun, moon, and stars, the earth and main,
Erewhile his portion, life and light,
To him exist in vain.

The clouds and sunbeams, o'er his eye
That once their shades and glory threw
Have left in yonder silent sky
No vestige where they flew.

The annals of the human race,
Their ruins, since the world began,
Of HIM afford no other trace
Than this, – THERE LIVED A MAN!

160   JAMES MONTGOMERY (1771–1854)

ANSWER TO A BEAUTIFUL POEM, WRITTEN BY MONTGOMERY, AUTHOR OF "THE WANDERER OF SWITZERLAND," ETC., ENTITLED "THE COMMON LOT."

Montgomery! true, the common lot
   Of mortals lies in Lethe's wave;
Yet some shall never be forgot,
   Some shall exist beyond the grave.

"Unknown the region of his birth,"
   The hero rolls the tide of war;
Yet not unknown his martial worth,
   Which glares a meteor from afar.

His joy or grief, his weal or woe,
   Perchance may 'scape the page of fame;
Yet nations, now unborn, will know
   The record of his deathless name.

The Patriot's and the Poet's frame
   Must share the common tomb of all:
Their glory will not sleep the same;
   "That" will arise, though Empires fall.

The lustre of a Beauty's eye
   Assumes the ghastly stare of death;

The fair, the brave, the good must die,
    And sink the yawning grave beneath.

Once more, the speaking eye revives,
    Still beaming through the lover's strain;
For Petrarch's Laura still survives:
    She died, but ne'er will die again.

The rolling seasons pass away,
    And Time, untiring, waves his wing;
Whilst honour's laurels ne'er decay,
    But bloom in fresh, unfading spring.

All, all must sleep in grim repose,
    Collected in the silent tomb;
The old, the young, with friends and foes,
    Fest'ring alike in shrouds, consume.

The mouldering marble lasts its day,
    Yet falls at length an useless fane;
To Ruin's ruthless fangs a prey,
    The wrecks of pillar'd Pride remain.

What, though the sculpture be destroy'd,
    From dark Oblivion meant to guard;
A bright renown shall be enjoy'd,
    By those, whose virtues claim reward.

Then do not say the common lot
  Of all lies deep in Lethe's wave;
Some few who ne'er will be forgot
  Shall burst the bondage of the grave.

EPITAPH ON AN ARMY OF MERCENARIES

These, in the day when heaven was falling,
    The hour when earth's foundations fled,
Followed their mercenary calling
    And took their wages, and are dead.
Their shoulders held the sky suspended;
    They stood, and earth's foundations stay;
What God abandoned, these defended,
    And saved the sum of things for pay.

ANOTHER EPITAPH ON AN ARMY
OF MERCENARIES

It is a God-damned lie to say that these
Saved, or knew, anything worth any man's pride.
They were professional murderers and they took
Their blood money and impious risks and died.
In spite of all their kind some elements of worth
With difficulty persist here and there on earth.

A THIRD EPITAPH ON AN ARMY
OF MERCENARIES

We write our own; no one does it for us.
Only those who have been there know the score.
The pay was good, but thousands more before us
Would testify note-counting's but a chore.

Adrenalin, adrenalin that courses
Along the blood as bullets do's the key.
Shouts, cracks, burning buildings were the sources
Of the hot joy that made us die – or dee.

A PACT

I make a pact with you, Walt Whitman —
I have detested you long enough.
I come to you as a grown child
Who has had a pig-headed father;
I am old enough now to make friends.
It was you that broke the new wood,
Now is a time for carving.
We have one sap and one root —
Let there be commerce between us.

EZRA POUND (1885–1972)

ANOTHER PACT

You've cowed me long enough, Ezra, with your red
    beard and fascist eyes.
I don't need you to teach me *How to Read*.
Tom Sawyer did that years before I'd heard of you.

I skipped the troubadours, that's true;
I was too busy fronting bands for fifteen years.
Your friend Bill Williams swears that, for all your talk
    of music, you were tone-deaf.
Ha! The way you threw Greek in my face, I hurl your
    tin ear back at you.

Call it *slush* and *slither* if you will – I love Romance.
I don't *go in fear of abstractions*; I love to mix them –
    like the concept of gravel – with the concrete.
I love to say "the Everest of your arrogance."
Too much *hard imagery* cracks teeth, then (as you
    know too well), the head.
I'd rather *make it nude*. Or *gnu*.

Shake your puppet-fists all day, Phineas T. Bluster
    of poesy –
I still prefer big trout to Dante, Cavalcanti, Bert de
    Born, or you.
I prefer Led Zeppelin, and the Minister of Silly Walks.
I prefer to scuba dive.

I've hovered – swaying with kelp forests, urchins
      brandishing black spikes below –
and watched my breath fizz up like soda bubbles
      toward the orange mouth of the sun.
I breathe easy at eighty feet, but choke when you start
      wheezing in my ear.

I'm just as serious as you.

My first guitar teacher, Mr. Schwartz, had wooden
      feet and a personality like hives.
He nettled me until I played scales perfectly, but
      feared to improvise.
Thanks for the lessons, Ez, whether I asked or not.
You gave your best. Now I can too.

CHARLES HARPER WEBB (1952–)   169

A KNOCKER

There are those who grow
gardens in their heads
paths lead from their hair
to sunny and white cities

it's easy for them to write
they close their eyes
immediately schools of images
stream down their foreheads

my imagination
is a piece of board
my sole instrument
is a wooden stick

I strike the board
it answers me
yes – yes
no – no

for others the green bell of a tree
the blue bell of water
I have a knocker
from unprotected gardens

I thump on the board
and it prompts me
with the moralist's dry poem
yes – yes
no – no

WE ALL KNOCK

You would strike a board
knock – knock
with thud of gaveled fist
until it answers –

a dry clucking,
no – no
like the clicking of brown sticks –
the imagination stripped,
austere as stone,

and would insist
that this is clarity –
where the river turns
to mud and brittle vegetation,
where dogs sniff;

have us think that beauty
is an easy stream that springs
from the head
effortlessly,
gurgling like a child,
sun-garnished
under a blue bell of sky;

not this *rapping, rapping,*
rapping that I do,
of wood
back to a trunk's concentric rings,
roots kneading into earth,
muscling into soil, until
it will sustain

that bell of green,
that spread of sky;
yes — yes

OATMEAL

I eat oatmeal for breakfast.
I make it on the hot plate and put skimmed milk on it.
I eat it alone.
I am aware it is not good to eat oatmeal alone.
Its consistency is such that it is better for your mental
      health if somebody eats it with you.
That is why I often think up an imaginary companion
      to have breakfast with.
Possibly it is even worse to eat oatmeal with an
      imaginary companion.
Nevertheless, yesterday morning, I ate my oatmeal
      with John Keats.
Keats said I was absolutely right to invite him: due to
      its glutinous texture, gluey lumpishness, hint of
      slime, and unsual willingness to disintegrate,
      oatmeal must never be eaten alone.
He said that in his opinion, however, it is OK to eat it
      with an imaginary companion,
and that he himself had enjoyed memorable porridges
      with Edmund Spenser and John Milton.
Even if such porridges are not as wholesome as Keats
      claims, still, you can learn something from them.
Yesterday morning, for instance, Keats told me about
      writing the "Ode to a Nightingale."
He had a heck of a time finishing it – those were his

words – "Oi 'ad a 'eck of a toime," he said, more or
    less, speaking through his porridge.
He wrote it quickly, on scraps of paper, which he then
    stuck in his pocket,
but when he got home he couldn't figure out the order
    of the stanzas, and he and a friend spread the papers
    on a table, and they made some sense of them, but
    he isn't sure to this day if they got it right.
He still wonders about the occasional sense of drift
    between stanzas,
and the way here and there a line will go into the
    configuration of a Moslem at prayer, then raise
    itself up and peer about, and then lay itself down
    slightly off the mark, causing the poem to move
    forward with God's reckless wobble.
He said someone told him that later in life
    Wordsworth heard about the scraps of paper on
    the table, and tried shuffling some stanzas of his
    own but only made matters worse.
When breakfast was over, John recited "To Autumn."
He recited it slowly, with much feeling, and he
    articulated the words lovingly, and his odd accent
    sounded sweet.
He didn't offer the story of writing "To Autumn,"
    I doubt if there is much of one.

But he did say the sight of a just-harvested oat field
    got him started on it
and two of the lines, "For Summer has o'er-brimmed
    their clammy cells" and "Thou watchest the last
    oozings hours by hours," came to him while
    eating oatmeal alone.
I can see him – drawing a spoon through the stuff,
    gazing into the glimmering furrows, muttering –
    and it occurs to me:
maybe there is no sublime, only the shining of the
    amnion's tatters.
For supper tonight I am going to have a baked potato
    left over from lunch.
I am aware that a leftover baked potato is damp, slippery,
    and simultaneously gummy and crumbly,
and therefore I'm going to invite Patrick Kavanagh to
    join me.

EATING OATMEAL

I don't know whether it's just the picture
of him in my book of contemporary
American poetry with pieces
of hair stuck onto his head like glue and
his grinning in spite of it – that I dislike
Galway Kinnell so. I don't like his poems
either. They often read like Russell Baker.
Take his poem "Oatmeal" about his imaginary
encounter with John Keats (who also eats
Oatmeal). One morning at breakfast Galway
is making Oatmeal on a hot plate and
putting skimmed milk on it. He is eating
it alone, when John Keats joins him for a
bowl. (Keats has enjoyed memorable porridge
himself with Edmund Spenser and John Milton.)
And Keats tells him about writing
"Ode to a Nightingale" and how he had
"a heck of a toime finishing it."
Keats speaks in a Cockney accent with his
mouth full of Oatmeal. He wrote it quickly
on scraps of paper, which he then stuck in
his pocket, where an entire stanza may have
slipped through a hole into the lining.
Galway often wonders about the occasional drift
of sense between the stanzas. I can see

Galway drawing a spoon through the stuff with
its gluey, glutinous texture and hint of
slime, and gazing into the glimmery furrows –
the presumptions of his poem making me mad.
I know it's a serious poem about writing.
I just dislike it for personal reasons. But
I wouldn't join him for a baked potato.
Thou wast not born for death, immortal Bird!

RONDEAU REDOUBLÉ

There are so many kinds of awful men –
One can't avoid them all. She often said
She'd never make the same mistake again:
She always made a new mistake instead.

The chinless type who made her feel ill-bred;
The practised charmer, less than charming when
He talked about the wife and kids and fled –
There are so many kinds of awful men.

The half-crazed hippy, deeply into Zen,
Whose cryptic homilies she came to dread;
The fervent youth who worshipped Tony Benn –
"One can't avoid them all," she often said.

The ageing banker, rich and overfed,
Who held forth on the dollar and the yen –
Though there were many more mistakes ahead,
She'd never make the same mistake again.

The budding poet, scribbling in his den
Odes not to her but to his pussy, Fred;
The drunk who fell asleep at nine or ten –
She always made a new mistake instead.

And so the gambler was at least unwed
And didn't preach or sneer or wield a pen
Or hoard his wealth or take the Scotch to bed.
She'd lived and learned and lived and learned but then
There are so many kinds.

REBUTTAL

There are so many kinds of tasty men.
I'm married now, but I still like to stare.
What use is there in trying to pretend?
Look at those handsome brothers strutting there –

those eyes, those lips, those hands, that style,
    that hair –
so fine that I can hardly apprehend
what's going on beneath that underwear.
There are so many kinds of tasty men,

both black and white, and then there are the blends –
the cocoa-brown or coffee-colored flair
of men even ex-girlfriends recommend.
I'm married now, but I still like to stare.

No way that I'll be having an affair
but oh my God, look at them preen and bend
in business suits or sweats – all debonair.
What use is there in trying to pretend,

as if my marriage marked the sorry end
of stirring underneath my skin, the bare
truth of libido, desire I'll defend.
Look at those handsome brothers strutting there!

How nice of them to walk on by, to share
this wealth I'm glad to have a chance to spend.
Excuse me while I go and get some air –
this kind of chemistry I comprehend.
There are so many kinds.

HOMAGES

"THEY FLEE FROM ME THAT SOMETIME DID ME SEEK"

They flee from me that sometime did me seek
    With naked foot stalking in my chamber.
I have seen them gentle tame and meek
    That now are wild and do not remember
    That sometime they put themselves in danger
To take bread at my hand; and now they range
Busily seeking with continual change.

Thank'd be fortune, it hath been otherwise
    Twenty times better; but once in special,
In thin array after a pleasant guise,
    When her loose gown from her shoulders did fall,
    And she me caught in her arms long and small,
Therewith all sweetly did me kiss,
And softly said, *Dear heart, how like you this?*

It was no dream: I lay broad waking.
    But all is turned through my gentleness
Into a strange fashion of forsaking;
    And I have leave to go of her goodness,
    And she also to use new-fangleness.
But since that I so kindely am served,
I would fain know what she hath deserved.

SIR THOMAS WYATT (1503–42)   185

BEFORE TIME

On one or two occasions
It was different: she lingered

At the window, turned – I was
Desirable because for a moment

I was anybody. The distance
Seemed to disappear without us
Moving but more than what followed

I remember the open window.
Taxis idling by the park.
Streetlights shining

Through the hemlock and the usual sounds
Of traffic, shouts – all of it
Starkly present and at the same time

Incomplete; as if a space I'd never
Wanted had been filled

At the moment
I wanted it: branches

Swirling at the window as
Her clothing dropped
To the floor. If I have chance

To thank for this moment
I'd like to know what she deserved.

JAMES LONGENBACH (1959–)   187

HOLY SONNET XIV

Batter my heart, three person'd God; for, you
As yet but knock, breathe, shine, and seek to mend;
That I may rise, and stand, o'erthrow me, and bend
Your force, to break, blow, burn and make me new.
I, like an usurp'd town, to' another due,
Labour to admit you, but Oh, to no end,
Reason your viceroy in me, me should defend,
But is captiv'd, and proves weak or untrue.
Yet dearly I love you, and would be loved fain,
But am betroth'd unto your enemy:
Divorce me, untie, or break that knot again,
Take me to you, imprison me, for I
Except you enthral me, never shall be free,
Nor ever chaste, except you ravish me.

UNHOLY SONNET

Soften the blow, imagined God, and give
Me one good reason for this punishment.
Where does the pressure come from? Is it meant
To kill me in the end or help me live?
My thoughts about you are derivative.
Still, I believe a part of me is bent
To make your grace look like an accident
And keep my soul from being operative.
But if I'm to be bent back like the pole
A horseshoe clangs against and gives a kink to,
Then take me like the grinning iron monger
I saw once twist a bar that made him sink to
His knees. His tongue was like a hot pink coal
As he laughed and said he thought that he was stronger.

A VALEDICTION: FORBIDDING MOURNING

As virtuous men pass mildly away,
    And whisper to their souls to go,
Whilst some of their sad friends do say,
    The breath goes now, and some say, no:

So let us melt, and make no noise,
    No tear-floods, nor sigh-tempests move,
'Twere profanation of our joys
    To tell the laity our love.

Moving of th' Earth brings harms and fears,
    Men reckon what it did and meant;
But trepidation of the spheres,
    Though greater far, is innocent.

Dull sublunary lovers' love
    (Whose soul is sense) cannot admit
Absence, because it doth remove
    Those things which elemented it.

But we by a love so much refined
    That ourselves know not what it is,
Inter-assurèd of the mind,
    Care less, eyes, lips, and hands to miss.

190

Our two souls therefore, which are one,
　　Though I must go, endure not yet
A breach, but an expansion,
　　Like gold to aery thinness beat.

If they be two, they are two so
　　As stiff twin compasses are two;
Thy soul the fixed foot makes no show
　　To move, but doth, if th' other do.

And though it in the centre sit,
　　Yet when the other far doth roam
It leans, and hearkens after it,
　　And grows erect as that comes home.

Such wilt thou be to me, who must
　　Like th' other foot obliquely run;
Thy firmness makes my circle just,
　　And makes me end where I begun.

AFTER VALEDICTIONS

The Love Poem is tricky –
not the least given Donne's

stiff conceits,

the mathematical intentions,
the gold to airy thinness beat.

What a challenge!
I have my whiny villanelle

on a previous marriage:
images of passing out – after what?

four or five kamikaze?

Then after meeting you – a sonnet
sanctioning tunnel, burrow, nest

as a version of *one*.

Certainly, for all the decades before we met
in the sublunary xerox closet

(I was forty, you were forty-seven –)

we can figure the forbidding circle as *won*.
Listen, the only place I'm going is the kitchen

or bed –
and so you will follow, my alchemical beloved.

PRAYER (I)

Prayer the Church's banquet, angels' age,
    God's breath in man returning to his birth,
    The soul in paraphrase, heart in pilgrimage,
The Christian plummet sounding heav'n and earth;
Engine against th' Almighty, sinner's tower,
    Reversed thunder, Christ-side-piercing spear,
    The six-days-world transposing in an hour,
A kind of tune, which all things hear and fear;
Softness, and peace, and joy, and love, and bliss,
    Exalted manna, gladness of the best,
    Heaven in ordinary, man well drest,
The milky way, the bird of paradise,
    Church-bells beyond the stars heard, the soul's blood,
    The land of spices; something understood.

GEORGE HERBERT (1593–1633)

SEPTEMBER 11

Understanding something isn't prayer, necessarily.

Cinnamon croissants, hot pretzels speared under glass,
cafe latte behind hostility's headlines. God

in the details: man well-dressed, reversed thunder
from a milky-breathed baby. Engines pitted against

time, take-off code from the air traffic control tower,
radar plumbing the atmosphere. Slumped in blue jean

bell-bottoms, teens nodding to heavy metal on ear
    phones.
Hard not to hear. Journey of strangers locked in a tube.

Annals of the absurd faithful, prepared to meet the stars
in a biff of pressured air. Softness of cruising, bliss

of landing, love waiting in the wings, the cockpit.
In ordinary hearts, a slivered wish. Muted joy

at unfastening seatbelts. Paraphrased as relief.
Flying from ice pole to desert to birders' paradise

in privileged pilgrimage, the best cuts of wool.
Storing luggage in the overheads, not knowing

the six days world would be transposed in one hour.

ON A DROP OF DEW

See how the orient dew,
Shed from the bosom of the morn
 Into the blowing roses,
Yet careless of its mansion new,
For the clear region where 'twas born
 Round in itself incloses,
 And in its little globe's extent
Frames as it can its native element;
How it the purple flower does slight,
 Scarce touching where it lies,
But gazing back upon the skies,
 Shines with a mournful light
  Like its own tear,
Because so long divided from the sphere.
 Restless it rolls and unsecure,
  Trembling lest it grow impure,
 Till the warm sun pity its pain,
And to the skies exhale it back again.
  So the soul, that drop, that ray
Of the clear fountain of eternal day,
Could it within the human flower be seen,
  Rememb'ring still its former height,
  Shuns the sweet leaves and blossoms green;
  And recollecting its own light,
Does, in its pure and circling thoughts, express

The greater heaven in an heaven less.
    In how coy a figure wound,
    Every way it turns away;
    So the world excluding round,
    Yet receiving in the day;
    Dark beneath but bright above,
    Here disdaining, there in love;
    How loose and easy hence to go,
    How girt and ready to ascend;
    Moving but on a point below,
    It all about does upwards bend.
Such did the manna's sacred dew distil,
White and entire, though congealed and chill;
Congealed on earth, but does, dissolving, run
Into the glories of th' almighty sun.

ON A DROP OF RAIN

Late in the day, the rain abating,
I force myself outside for my daily walk.
I do not go far. Everything is doused
And diamonded with water. Even the stones
Seem polished. At each bud of every scrub
Roadside tree, and even on the thorns
Of wild roses, hangs a drop of rain –
As if someone had hoisted chandeliers
To light the road from end to end.

I think of Marvell, how he found a story
One morning shining with meaning
In a drop of dew. A figure for the soul,
Marvell's dewdrop contained the whole
Sky and, mindful of its native home,
Came and went, scarcely touching
The earthly flower on which it floated,
Its one aspiration the sunny exhalation
Of water into air. It never seemed to feel

Death's shiver. Here, it's nearly evening,
The air still rheumy enough to silver
The weedy edge of the road where beer cans
Find their rest. My raindrops – tense, trembling –
Really do seem to cling for dear life,

A story, I'm sad to say, of my all too earthly
Wish to hang around forever in my body.
No chance, the wind says, extinguishing
With every breeze, one drop after another.

"WHY – DO THEY SHUT ME OUT OF HEAVEN?"

Why – do they shut Me out of Heaven?
Did I sing – too loud?
But – I can say a little "Minor"
Timid as a Bird!

Wouldn't the Angels try me –
Just – once – more –
Just – see – if I troubled them –
But don't – shut the door!

Oh, if I – were the Gentleman
In the "White Robe" –
And they – were the little Hand – that knocked –
Could – I – forbid?

EMILY DICKINSON (1830–86)

SAY A LITTLE "MINOR"

Make me listen. It's your stubbornness
I love: The way your song breaks out – the hell with
it (those jealous flames, your loneliness) –
the way you bend your blues note down. No melody.

Beloved jay, thrush, finch, lark dust:
No bird form piercing gloom is timid. Cagey,
aren't you, feathered thing, or were you tossed
out, cursed, then uncursed by the very language
coursing through you? This stubbornness. Just
whispering, it finds its way. It must.

"LOVELIEST OF TREES,
THE CHERRY NOW"

Loveliest of trees, the cherry now
Is hung with bloom along the bough,
And stands about the woodland ride
Wearing white for Eastertide.

Now, of my threescore years and ten,
Twenty will not come again,
And take from seventy springs a score,
It only leaves me fifty more.

And since to look at things in bloom
Fifty springs are little room,
About the woodlands I will go
To see the cherry hung with snow.

A. E. HOUSMAN (1859–1936)

PUTTING ON THE RITZ
For William Jules-Yves

After a long, cool winter,
at last in May a suite
of warm days wakes the sleepers.

One covered from crown to root
in thick crepe skirtlets stops
me, back from hibernation:

Loveliest of trees,
big as the Ritz's balletic
vases charged with bloom.

Not bought, not concocted,
only improbably real.
Why am I not surprised?

My hair is snowed with silver,
evidence how little room
fifty springs allow.

And yet midwinter someone
burst to life inside me,
and lately started dancing.

Just so improbably
snow hung along the branches
changed suddenly to flowers.

THE CUCUMBER

To Ekber Babayev

The snow is knee-deep in the courtyard
and still coming down hard:
it hasn't let up all morning.
We're in the kitchen.
On the table, on the oilcloth, spring –
on the table there's a very tender young cucumber,
                              pebbly and fresh as a daisy.
We're sitting around the table staring at it.
It softly lights up our faces,
and the very air smells fresh.
We're sitting around the table staring at it,
amazed
          thoughtful
                        optimistic.
We're as if in a dream.
On the table, on the oilcloth, hope –
on the table, beautiful days,
a cloud seeded with a green sun,
an emerald crowd impatient and on its way,
loves blooming openly –
on the table, there on the oilcloth, a very tender young
    cucumber,

                              pebbly and fresh as a daisy.

The snow is knee-deep in the courtyard
and coming down hard.
It hasn't let up all morning.

204   NAZIM HIKMET (1902–63)
TRANSLATED BY RANDY BLASING AND
MUTLU KONUK

CONNECTICUT THANKS YOU, NAZIM

On the yard of Danbury Women's Prison,
on the steps of Westerly Terrace Wallace
Stevens walked down, sleeptalking his poem,
on the orchards and peach trees of Silverman's
Farm and the tented rows of roller leaf tobacco
and the wide green lawns that flow into
the Sound like the Mississippi River,
the snow falls much the same.

Thank you, Nazim, for reminding us of
the fairness of snow and hope after
the unfairness of your life, imprisoned
with only the memory of cigarettes,
apples and clean white shirts and the secrets
of the simple cucumber you came to celebrate
at the expense of your freedom.

THE BLACK SWAN

When the swans turned my sister into a swan
    I would go to the lake, at night, from milking:
The sun would look out through the reeds like a swan,
    A swan's red beak; and the beak would open
And inside there was darkness, the stars and the moon.

Out on the lake a girl would laugh.
    "Sister, here is your porridge, sister,"
I would call; and the reeds would whisper,
    "Go to sleep, go to sleep, little swan."
My legs were all hard and webbed, and the silky

Hairs of my wings sank away like stars
    In the ripples that ran in and out of the reeds:
I heard through the lap and hiss of water
    Someone's "Sister . . . sister," far away on the shore,
And then as I opened my beak to answer

I heard my harsh laugh go out to the shore
    And saw – saw at last, swimming up from the green
Low mounds of the lake, the white stone swans:
    The white, named swans . . . "It is all a dream,"
I whispered, and reached from the down of the pallet

To the lap and hiss of the floor.
    And "Sleep, little sister," the swans all sang
From the moon and stars and frogs of the floor.
    But the swan my sister called, "Sleep at last,
        little sister,"
And stroked all night, with a black wing, my wings.

THE BLUE-EYED WIFE

When the buzzards turned my husband into a buzzard,
    I stood in the fields and watched them glide.
Their pinions caressed the white skin of my throat.
    Their strength circled, tilted, and slid into me
Until we hung there like kites in a gorge of air.

And then I was freed from the duties of milking,
    Of feeding the old ones now the young ones are gone.
Their faces were hooded with crimson ribbons,
    And their bones were thrown in the marly loam
Of Borrow Pit, turning white in a white leprous foam.

He comes at the dead of night to watch me breathe –
    When my eyelids quiver, I am dreaming of flight.
Then shadows move and long wings double – he blots
    Out the stars, overshadows my feathers. I shudder,
My eyes black with a hunger that can never be eased.

YOUNG SYCAMORE

I must tell you
this young tree
whose round and firm trunk
between the wet

pavement and the gutter
(where water
is trickling) rises
bodily

into the air with
one undulant
thrust half its height –
and then

dividing and waning
sending out
young branches on
all sides –

hung with cocoons –
it thins
till nothing is left of it
but two

eccentric knotted
twigs
bending forward
hornlike at the top

WILLIAM CARLOS WILLIAMS (1883–1963)   209

OLD SYCAMORE

In memory of
Joel Oppenheimer, 1930–88

The slender young
sycamores of Rutherford,
New Jersey, are fat

now, trunks
scarred, half dead,
no longer

there. The poems
Williams left

behind, always new
in themselves,

are old
too. What I fear
is that our
language,

possessed
of so much

light that it
has filled
the world with

things
we *must* be
told of,

now
battered by
decades of
persuasion,

can no longer
make a thing
so clear I am

overwhelmed by
its clarity, can

no longer make
a thing into
a word spoken

once and within
that single
utterance

repeated, over
and over, until
it reaches, then

exceeds its own
self-meaning
and we lose

sight
of it, begin
to see instead,
everything around

it – a whole
world of new

things made from
an old thing
brought into

being in one
single beat

of existence
– the offering,
then, of a

thing
left behind.

THEME FOR ENGLISH B

The instructor said,

> *Go home and write*
> *a page tonight.*
> *And let that page come out of you —*
> *Then, it will be true.*

I wonder if it's that simple?
I am twenty-two, colored, born in Winston-Salem.
I went to school there, then Durham, then here
to this college on the hill above Harlem.
I am the only colored student in my class.
The steps from the hill lead down into Harlem,
through a park, then I cross St. Nicholas,
Eighth Avenue, Seventh, and I come to the Y,
the Harlem Branch Y, where I take the elevator
up to my room, sit down, and write this page:

It's not easy to know what is true for you or me
at twenty-two, my age. But I guess I'm what
I feel and see and hear, Harlem, I hear you:
hear you, hear me — we two — you, me, talk on this page.
(I hear New York, too.) Me — who?
Well, I like to eat, sleep, drink, and be in love.
I like to work, read, learn, and understand life.

I like a pipe for a Christmas present,
or records – Bessie, bop, or Bach.
I guess being colored doesn't make me *not* like
the same things other folks like who are other races.
So will my page be colored that I write?
Being me, it will not be white.
But it will be
a part of you, instructor.
You are white –
yet a part of me, as I am a part of you.
That's American.
Sometimes perhaps you don't want to be a part of me.
Nor do I often want to be a part of you.
But we are, that's true!
As I learn from you,
I guess you learn from me –
although you're older – and white –
and somewhat more free.

This is my page for English B.

THEME FOR INTERMEDIATE CHINESE
After Langston Hughes' "Theme for English B"

Teacher recites and I follow, copying her words
Taping the class so I can listen at home *make sentences*
She says one for every word and I count them
In Chinese, building the tones from memories

A child of the fifties, it is the time of my fifties
When I rub my hair and touch only the wrinkly skin
That has forgotten hair . . . I count days as gifts now
Homework is a gift and this small flat twelve
        thousand miles
Away, on the other side of forgetting and remembering

I take the MRT subway to my neighborhood
Walk past the lady who is not so nice to the faces
        that warm
And brighten when I pass, through the park with
        children
Slides swings and old women under the trees
Across the tiles of the walkway to my building to press
My security key to the elevator, kiss it softly to say
It's me again as if the key doesn't know the only black man
In the neighborhood

我

is the word for "I" and it sounds like woe's sadness,
Or whoa, the sound to stop the whirring of things
I practice it, writing over and over, rolling on the sound
Of the elevated train going by . . . where everyone knows
    I *is* me
I meditate on the congregation of genes and wishes
That brought me here, counting back the four
    generations
To the first African, naming along the way the Native
    Americans
Europeans the polka dot army of chromosomes and
    molecules
Like tiny space ships that align themselves with
    mystic glue
So that I am the same mystery each day and do not
    dissolve
Into a glob in the midst of Taipei's rush to go and
    buy things
As I recite alone to myself the Chinese for going and
    buying

What have I bought in this place where only the inside
Can matter and the outside is so many things to so many
And who are we? The Chinese sentence for this takes me

All night, into the slide of constellations over night
    markets
And the humid cling of music to silence . . . we are genes
We are the art of the mind of some great emptiness above
Or here below inside the bulb of a beet, things that grow
Underground and thrive on darkness, the humble
    fullness of light.

A BLESSING

Just off the highway to Rochester, Minnesota,
Twilight bounds softly forth on the grass.
And the eyes of those two Indian ponies
Darken with kindness.
They have come gladly out of the willows
To welcome my friend and me.
We step over the barbed wire into the pasture
Where they have been grazing all day, alone.
They ripple tensely, they can hardly contain their
     happiness
That we have come.
They bow shyly as wet swans. They love each other.
There is no loneliness like theirs.
At home once more,
They begin munching the young tufts of spring in the
     darkness.
I would like to hold the slenderer one in my arms,
For she has walked over to me
And nuzzled my left hand.
She is black and white,
Her mane falls wild on her forehead,
And the light breeze moves me to caress her long ear
That is delicate as the skin over a girl's wrist.
Suddenly I realize
That if I stepped out of my body I would break
Into blossom.

SOURCE

I'd been traveling all day, driving north
— smaller and smaller roads, clapboard houses
startled awake by the new green around them —

when I saw three horses in a fenced field
by the narrow highway's edge: white horses,

two uniformly snowy, the other speckled
as though he'd been rolling in flakes of rust.
They were of graduated sizes

— small, medium, large — and two stood
to watch while the smallest waded

up to his knees in a shallow pond,
tossing his head and taking
— it seemed unmistakable — delight

in the cool water around his hooves
and ankles. I kept on driving, I went into town

to visit the bookstore and the coffee bar,
and looked at the new novels
and the volumes of poetry, but all the time

it was horses I was thinking of,
and when I drove back to find them

the three companions left off
whatever it was they were playing at,
and came nearer the wire fence –

I'd pulled over onto the grassy shoulder
of the highway – to see what I'd brought them.

Experience is an intact fruit,
core and flesh and rind of it; once cut open,
entered, it can't be the same, can it?

Though that is the dream of the poem:
as if we could look out

through that moment's blushed skin.
They wandered toward the fence.
The tallest turned toward me;

I was moved by the verticality of her face,
elongated reach from the ear-tips

down to white eyelids and lashes,
the pink articulation
of nostrils, wind stirring the strands

220

of her mane a little to frame the gaze
in which she fixed me. She was the bold one;

the others stood at a slight distance
while she held me in her attention.
Put your tongue to the green-flecked

peel of it, reader, and taste it
from the inside: Would you believe me
if I said that beneath them a clear channel

ran from the three horses to the place
they'd come from, the cool womb

of nothing, cave at the heart
of the world, deep and resilient and firmly set
at the core of things? Not emptiness,

not negation, but a generous, cold nothing:
the breathing space out of which new shoots

are propelled to the grazing mouths,
out of which horses themselves are tendered
into the new light. The poem wants the impossible;

the poem wants a name for the kind of nothing
at the core of time, out of which the foals

come tumbling: curled, fetal, dreaming,
and into which the old crumple, fetlock
and skull breaking like waves of foaming milk . . .

Cold, bracing nothing, which mothers forth
mud and mint, hoof and clover, root-hair

and horse-hair and the accordion bones
of the rust-spotted little one unfolding itself
into the afternoon. You too: you flare

and fall back into the necessary
open space. What could be better than that?

It was the beginning of May,
the black earth nearly steaming,
and a scatter of petals decked the mud

like pearls, everything warm with setting out,
and you could see beneath their hooves
the path they'd traveled up, the horse-road

on which they trot into the world, eager for pleasure
and sunlight, and down which they descend,

in good time, into the source of spring.

222   MARK DOTY (1953–)

THOSE WINTER SUNDAYS

Sundays too my father got up early
and put his clothes on in the blueblack cold,
then with cracked hands that ached
from labor in the weekday weather made
banked fires blaze. No one ever thanked him.

I'd wake and hear the cold splintering, breaking.
When the rooms were warm, he'd call,
and slowly I would rise and dress,
fearing the chronic angers of that house,

Speaking indifferently to him,
who had driven out the cold
and polished my good shoes as well.
What did I know, what did I know
of love's austere and lonely offices?

ROBERT HAYDEN (1913–80)

THOSE GEORGIA SUNDAYS

In Georgia, too, my father got up early,
wearing piss-stained boxers in the August heat,
then with yellow hands that reeked of *Vantage
Ultra Light 100s*, made the A/C shudder.

Jesus Fucking Christ, I'd thank him
as he moaned, hacking and spitting in the john.
And when the toaster clunked, slowly
I would rise and make the sofa-bed,

knowing we had no time left, yet saying
nothing to him, all the way to our weekend job
waxing floors at Southern Bell.

What did I know? I knew damned well.
And even over the hum I heard death hiss
through those austere and lonely offices.

PLAY

Nothing's going to become of anyone
except death:
   therefore: it's okay
to yearn
too high:
the grave accommodates
swell rambunctiousness &

ruin's not
compromised by magnificence:

that cut-off point
liberates us to the
common disaster: so
  pick a perch –
apple branch for example in bloom –
tune up
and

drill imagination right through necessity:
it's all right:
it's been taken care of:

is allowed, considering

A. R. AMMONS (1926–2001)

BECOMING

And so we are becoming
dead, you said
in a poem called *Play.*
You say *Okay*
to all our flights of fancy.
But beyond permission
for our *swell rambunctiousness*
is your piercing admonition:
drill imagination right through necessity:
as if play were as protestant
as work.

Now that you are one
who no longer walks among us,
what's become of you?
Do you still explore the bounds,
the edges and the sounds
of the distant shore? Each day
I read a poem or two
of yours, and I play with you:
becoming one
with you, very much alive.

A BOY GOES INTO THE WORLD

My brother rode off on his bike
into the summer afternoon, but
Mother called me back
from the end of the sandy drive:
"It's different for girls."

He'd be gone for hours, come back
with things: a cocoon, gray-brown
and papery around a stick;
a puff ball, ripe, wrinkled,
and exuding spores; owl pellets –
bits of undigested bone and fur;
and pieces of moss that might
have made toupees for preposterous
green men, but went instead
into a wide-necked jar for a terrarium.

He mounted his plunder on poster
board, gluing and naming
each piece. He has long since
forgotten those days and things, but
I at last can claim them as my own.

JANE KENYON (1947–95)   227

A GIRL GOES INTO THE WORLD

Never, did she say, "It's different for girls,"
not even when in fear she called the police
while I, lost in the forest, picked a way
through blackberry brambles hearing conversations
of last years' whispering dead beneath my feet
with the living in the wind above my head,
unaware that I should be afraid,
until I came to a road I knew and a neighbor
who'd been sent out to patrol and find me.
She wasn't even angry. She knew the price.
And yes, she knew it was a lie, her pretense
that a girl could have a boy's adventure,
safely. I believed. Bless her lie.
Bless her. Bless the lie that blessed me.

IN GOOD FUN

THE DESTRUCTION OF SENNACHERIB

The Assyrian came down like the wolf on the fold,
And his cohorts were gleaming in purple and gold;
And the sheen of their spears was like stars on the sea,
When the blue wave rolls nightly on deep Galilee.

Like the leaves of the forest when Summer is green,
That host with their banners at sunset were seen:
Like the leaves of the forest when Autumn hath blown,
That host on the morrow lay wither'd and strown.

For the Angel of Death spread his wings on the blast,
And breathed in the face of the foe as he pass'd;
And the eyes of the sleepers wax'd deadly and chill,
And their hearts but once heaved, and for ever grew still!

And there lay the steed with his nostril all wide,
But through it there roll'd not the breath of his pride;
And the foam of his gasping lay white on the turf,
And cold as the spray of the rock-beating surf.

And there lay the rider distorted and pale,
With the dew on his brow, and the rust on his mail:
And the tents were all silent, the banners alone,
The lances unlifted, the trumpet unblown.

And the widows of Ashur are loud in their wail,
And the idols are broke in the temple of Baal;
And the might of the Gentile, unsmote by the sword,
Hath melted like snow in the glance of the Lord!

VERY LIKE A WHALE

One thing that literature would be greatly the better for
Would be a more restricted employment by authors of
    simile and metaphor.
Authors of all races, be they Greeks, Romans, Teutons
    or Celts,
Can't seem just to say that anything is the thing it is
    but have to go out of their way to say it is like
    something else.
What does it mean when we are told
That the Assyrian came down like a wolf on the fold?
In the first place, George Gordon Byron had had enough
    experience
To know that it probably wasn't just one Assyrian, it was
    a *lot* of Assyrians.
However, as too many arguments are apt to induce
    apoplexy and thus hinder longevity,
We'll let it pass as one Assyrian for the sake of brevity.
Now then, this particular Assyrian, the one whose
    cohorts were gleaming in purple and gold,
Just what does the poet mean when he says he came
    down like a wolf on the fold?
In heaven and earth more than is dreamed of in our
    philosophy there are great many things,
But I don't imagine that among them there is a wolf with
    purple and gold cohorts or purple and gold
    anythings.

No, no, Lord Byron, before I'll believe that this Assyrian
was actually like a wolf I must have some kind of
proof;
Did he run on all fours and did he have a hairy tail and a
big red mouth and big white teeth and did he say
Woof woof woof?
Frankly I think it very unlikely, and all you were entitled
to say, at the very most,
Was that the Assyrian cohorts came down like a lot of
Assyrian cohorts about to destroy the Hebrew host.
But that wasn't fancy enough for Lord Byron, oh dear
me, no, he had to invent a lot of figures of speech
and then interpolate them,
With the result that whenever you mention Old
Testament soldiers to people they say Oh yes,
they're the ones that a lot of wolves dressed up in
gold and purple ate them.
That's the kind of thing that's being done all the time by
poets, from Homer to Tennyson;
They're always comparing ladies to lilies and veal to
venison,
And they always say things like that the snow is a white
blanket after a winter storm.
Oh it is, is it, all right then, you sleep under a six-inch
blanket of snow and I'll sleep under a half-inch
blanket of unpoetical blanket material and we'll see
which one keeps warm,
And after that maybe you'll begin to comprehend dimly
What I mean by too much metaphor and simile.

SONNET XLIII

How do I love thee? Let me count the ways.
I love thee to the depth and breadth and height
My soul can reach, when feeling out of sight
For the ends of Being and ideal Grace.
I love thee to the level of every day's
Most quiet need, by sun and candle-light.
I love thee freely, as men strive for Right;
I love thee purely, as they turn from Praise.
I love thee with the passion put to use
In my old griefs, and with my childhood's faith.
I love thee with a love I seemed to lose
With my lost saints, — I love thee with the breath,
Smiles, tears, of all my life! — and, if God choose,
I shall but love thee better after death.

ELIZABETH BARRETT BROWNING (1806–61)   235

OH, NOTHING

How do I love thee? Well, I don't really. I'm trapped
in penmanship that obfuscates the real. If you'd come
see me, a matrimony of touch would ensue, I'd unwrap
like a package for you, my ribbon wantonly unstrung

by fumbling fingers tugging the bow until I'm loose,
scotchtaped gift paper strewn all around the bedroom
like limp black stockings you may wear if you choose,
I'd peel them off you, then you'd be completely nude,

dazed and bashful, I presume, strung out. But let's see
how many more ways we can count this crazy-making
delay as if faking orgasm's fun. Uhm, it dawns on me

your unavailability may be a problem, I'm not shaking
dice for a reroll. I'm seriously concerned about time,
ticking languorously away. But, hey, you're busy,
        right?

DOVER BEACH

The sea is calm tonight.
The tide is full, the moon lies fair
Upon the Straits; – on the French coast, the light
Gleams and is gone; the cliffs of England stand,
Glimmering and vast, out in the tranquil bay.
Come to the window, sweet is the night air!
Only, from the long line of spray
Where the ebb meets the moon-blanch'd land,
Listen! you hear the grating roar
Of pebbles which the waves suck back, and fling,
At their return, up the high strand,
Begin, and cease, and then again begin,
With tremulous cadence slow, and bring
The eternal note of sadness in.

Sophocles long ago
Heard it on the Aegean, and it brought
Into his mind the turbid ebb and flow
Of human misery; we
Find also in the sound a thought,
Hearing it by this distant northern sea.

The Sea of Faith
Was once, too, at the full, and round earth's shore
Lay like the folds of a bright girdle furl'd.

But now I only hear
Its melancholy, long, withdrawing roar,
Retreating, to the breath
Of the night-wind, down the vast edges drear
And naked shingles of the world.

Ah, love, let us be true
To one another! for the world, which seems
To lie before us like a land of dreams,
So various, so beautiful, so new,
Hath really neither joy, nor love, nor light,
Nor certitude, nor peace, nor help for pain;
And we are here as on a darkling plain
Swept with confused alarms of struggle and flight,
Where ignorant armies clash by night.

238   MATTHEW ARNOLD (1822–88)

THE DOVER BITCH: A CRITICISM OF LIFE

So there stood Matthew Arnold and this girl
With the cliffs of England crumbling away behind them,
And he said to her, "Try to be true to me,
And I'll do the same for you, for things are bad
All over, etc., etc."
Well now, I knew this girl. It's true she had read
Sophocles in a fairly good translation
And caught that bitter allusion to the sea,
But all the time he was talking she had in mind
The notion of what his whiskers would feel like
On the back of her neck. She told me later on
That after a while she got to looking out
At the lights across the channel, and really felt sad,
Thinking of all the wine and enormous beds
And blandishments in French and the perfumes.
And then she got really angry. To have been brought
All the way down from London, and then be addressed
As a sort of mournful cosmic last resort
Is really tough on a girl, and she was pretty.
Anyway, she watched him pace the room
And finger his watch-chain and seem to sweat a bit,
And then she said one or two unprintable things.
But you mustn't judge her by that. What I mean to say is,
She's really all right. I still see her once in a while
And she always treats me right. We have a drink

And I give her a good time, and perhaps it's a year
Before I see her again, but there she is,
Running to fat, but dependable as they come,
And sometimes I bring her a bottle of *Nuit d'Amour*.

IT WILL BUT SHAKE & TOTTER

Many poems have been written about the turgid sea.
For instance: the one about the man & his lover on the
      cliffs above the turgid sea.
It is the English Channel
& he is Matthew Arnold in 1851.
Across from him: "ignorant armies," "clashing by night."

The armies are not French.
They may be stars if what we've always thought of
      as stars
turned out to be the fading chalk of a fading language,
turned out to be nothing but the small sparks of rocks
being struck by chains in the corners of the sky.

Like a Russian novel the sea roils & cedes, roils & cedes.
Fish do their fish-like work among its atavistic depths.
Notice how the moonlight glisters like lacquer
between the crests & troughs, the smell of the brine,
the heavy, salt-stung air.

All night the moon rings & rings.
All night the wind searches the cliffs for a flag,
a kite, a woman's hat.

Love, I say, let us be true. Let us be.
The world is but a darkling plain. A hill of beans.
We are the few & we are the far between.

SPENCER SHORT (1972–)   241

CANTO XLV

With Usura
With usura hath no man a house of good stone
each block cut smooth and well fitting
that design might cover their face,
with usura
hath no man a painted paradise on his church wall
harpes et luthes
or where virgin receiveth message
and halo projects from incision,
with usura
seeth no man Gonzaga his heirs and his concubines
no picture is made to endure nor to live with
but it is made to sell and sell quickly
with usura, sin against nature,
is thy bread ever more of stale rags
is thy bread dry as paper,
with no mountain wheat, no strong flour
with usura the line grows thick
with usura is no clear demarcation
and no man can find site for his dwelling.
Stone cutter is kept from his stone
weaver is kept from his loom
WITH USURA
wool comes not to market
sheep bringeth no gain with usura
Usura is a murrain, usura

blunteth the needle in the maid's hand
and stoppeth the spinner's cunning. Pietro Lombardo
came not by usura
Duccio came not by usura
nor Pier della Francesca; Zuan Bellin' not by usura
nor was "La Calunnia" painted.
Came not by usura Angelico; came not Ambrogio
    Praedis,
Came no church of cut stone signed: *Adamo me fecit.*
Not by usura Saint Trophime
Not by usura Saint Hilaire,
Usura rusteth the chisel
It rusteth the craft and the craftsman
It gnaweth the thread in the loom
None learneth to weave gold in her pattern;
Azure hath a canker by usura; cramoisi is unbroidered
Emerald findeth no Memling
Usura slayeth the child in the womb
It stayeth the young man's courting
It hath brought palsey to bed, lyeth
between the young bride and her bridegroom
                CONTRA NATURAM
They have brought whores for Eleusis
Corpses are set to banquet
at behest of usura.

EZRA POUND (1885–1972)

WITH TENURE

If Ezra Pound were alive today
            (and he is)
he'd be teaching
at a small college in the Pacific Northwest
and attending the annual convention
of writing instructors in St. Louis
and railing against tenure,
saying tenure
is a ladder whose rungs slip out
from under the scholar as he climbs
upwards to empty heaven
by the angels abandoned
for tenure killeth the spirit
(with tenure no man becomes master)
Texts are unwritten with tenure,
under the microscope, *sous rature*
it turneth the scholar into a drone
decayeth the pipe in his jacket's breast pocket.
Hamlet was not written with tenure,
nor were written Schubert's lieder
nor Manet's *Olympia* painted with tenure.
No man of genius rises by tenure
Nor woman (I see you smile).
Picasso came not by tenure
nor Charlie Parker;

Came not by tenure Wallace Stevens
Not by tenure Marcel Proust
Nor Turner by tenure
With tenure hath only the mediocre
a sinecure unto death. Unto death, I say!
WITH TENURE
Nature is constipated the sap doesn't flow
With tenure the classroom is empty
            et in academia ego
the ketchup is stuck inside the bottle
the letter goes unanswered the bell doesn't ring.

THIS IS JUST TO SAY

I have eaten
the plums
that were in
the icebox

and which
you were probably
saving
for breakfast

Forgive me
they were delicious
so sweet
and so cold

VARIATIONS ON A THEME BY
WILLIAM CARLOS WILLIAMS

1

I chopped down the house that you had been saving to
    live in next summer.
I am sorry, but it was morning, and I had nothing to do
and its wooden beams were so inviting.

2

We laughed at the hollyhocks together
and then I sprayed them with lye.
Forgive me. I simply do not know what I am doing.

3

I gave away the money that you had been saving to live
    on for the next ten years.
The man who asked for it was shabby
and the firm March wind on the porch was so juicy
    and cold.

4

Last evening we went dancing and I broke your leg.
Forgive me. I was clumsy, and
I wanted you here in the wards, where I am the doctor!

KENNETH KOCH (1925–2002)

SPECIAL THANKS

for those who led us in the right direction

Rachel Simon
Laure-Anne Bosselaar
Jonathan Aaron
David Fenza
Steve Huff
Marvin Bell
Richard Foerster
Estha Weiner
Michael Collier
Peter Wood

ACKNOWLEDGMENTS

Thanks are due to the following copyright holders for permission to reprint:

A. R. AMMONS: "Play" from *Collected Poems 1951–1971* by A. R. Ammons. Copyright © 1972 by A. R. Ammons. Used by permission of W. W. Norton & Company, Inc. W. H. AUDEN: "Musée des Beaux Arts", copyright 1940 & renewed 1968 by W. H. Auden, from *Collected Poems* by W. H. Auden. Used by permission of Random House, Inc. "Musée des Beaux Arts" by W. H. Auden, from *Collected Poems*. Reprinted with permission from Faber & Faber. COLEMAN BARKS: "Unmarked Boxes" from *Open Secrets* by Rumi, translated by Coleman Barks © 1984. Used by arrangement with Shambhala Publications Inc., Boston, MA. www.shambhala.com MARVIN BELL: "Variations on a Theme by Wordsworth" by Marvin Bell. Reprinted from *Prairie Schooner*, volume 80, number 2 (summer 2006) by permission of the University of Nebraska Press. Copyright 2006 University of Nebraska Press. BRUCE BERGER: "Casabianca III", previously unpublished and included with permission. ELIZABETH BISHOP: "Casabianca" by Elizabeth Bishop, from *Complete Poems*. Reprinted with permission from Farrar, Straus & Giroux. JOHN BERRYMAN: "Dream Song 171" (18 lines) from *Dream Songs* by John Berryman. Reprinted with permission of Faber & Faber and Farrar, Straus & Giroux. STAR BLACK: "Oh, Nothing" by Star Black. Reprinted by kind permission of the author. TERESA CADER: "September 11" by Teresa Cader, first published in *Slate*, September 2002. Reprinted with permission of the author. CHRISTINE CASSON: "We All Knock" by Christine Casson. Reprinted by kind permission of the author. CATULLUS (trans. Charles Martin): "Two Fragments" by Catullus. Martin, Charles, trans. *The Poems of Catullus*, pp. 41, 107. © 1989 The John Hopkins University Press. Reprinted with permission of